Everyday Elevation

A DAILY DOSE OF INSPIRATION TO SET YOURSELF FREE

xo ~ YVETTE ~ xo

Copyright © 2024 Yvette
All rights reserved
First Edition

PAGE PUBLISHING
Conneaut Lake, PA

First originally published by Page Publishing 2024

ISBN 979-8-89315-245-6 (pbk)
ISBN 979-8-89315-267-8 (digital)

Printed in the United States of America

I dedicate this inspirational book to the incredible women in my life: my mother, who brought me into this world; my two sisters, whom I look up to every day; and my three daughters, whom I've nurtured and guided toward a prosperous, vibrant, and positive life. Thank you all for being by my side. I love you dearly.

JANUARY

Embark on a New Year, Rejuvenate, and Seize Control of Your Journey

January 1: A day to celebrate a new year, not burdened by unnecessary pressure and anxiety from unattainable commitments.

Instead of piling on resolutions, consider the joy in completing even the smallest tasks left lingering from the past year. It's not about setting lofty goals but relishing in the satisfaction of accomplishments.

Much like an artist who cannot fully articulate a masterpiece until it's finished, the beauty lies in the process and culmination of effort. This new year, let the emphasis shift from what needs to be accomplished to what has already been achieved. Take a moment to appreciate the steps, big or small, that have led you to this point.

Consider the wisdom in finishing what you started, tying up loose ends before forging ahead. A clean slate isn't just about what's ahead but also about the clarity that comes from concluding what's behind. It's a time for reflection, gratitude, and acknowledging the progress made, no matter how incremental.

So as you step into this new chapter, don't be in a hurry to set ambitious goals. Instead, savor the sense of accomplishment in the completion of tasks that often go unnoticed. Celebrate the victories, no matter how small, and let the new year be a canvas where each stroke contributes to a masterpiece in the making.

January 2: The celebration does not have to end.

Remember, a number is only a number; it holds no power unless we assign it meaning. So as you embrace the beginning of this new year, carry the spirit of celebration forward. Recognize that the essence of a fresh start extends beyond the first day.

So as the second day of the year unfolds, carry the celebration with you. Embrace the power of collaboration, navigate challenges with grace, and remember that the pursuit of organized living is a journey worth taking, not just for yourself but for the collective well-being.

January 3: Shine bright like the star you are.

Today is not just another day; it's an opportunity to radiate your brilliance. As the sun rises, so does your potential. Let's embark on this journey with purpose and enthusiasm.

So shine bright, get organized, stay motivated, and let the inspiration within you guide the way. Today is not just another day; it's a chance to illuminate your path and inspire others to do the same.

January 4: You are stronger than you think.

As the days unfold, it's crucial to recognize the reservoir of strength within you. Life's journey may be challenging, but your resilience is a force to be reckoned with. Today, let's reaffirm your inner power and keep pushing forward toward the life you envision.

January 5: Embrace your freedom.

On this day, liberate yourself to be unapologetically you. Break free from the confines of conventionality, and let your thoughts soar beyond the limits of the box. Fear not the unknown; instead, view it as an opportunity for growth. Dare to take risks that propel you toward new horizons. Today, make a conscious choice to challenge yourself, transcending the boundaries of fear. In doing so, discover the boundless potential that awaits when you embrace the freedom to be authentically and courageously you.

January 6: Harness the power of positivity.

On this day, recognize the profound impact of positive energy. Banish the frowns, and instead, let a smile illuminate your path. In the face of challenges, flip that frown upside down and propel yourself toward what truly ignites your passion. Let positivity be the driving force that propels you forward, infusing every step with enthusiasm and determination. Today, embrace the transformative power of a positive mindset and set forth toward what fuels your inner fire.

January 7: Discover inner beauty.

On this day, uncover the intrinsic beauty within and extend the search to find goodness in everyone you encounter. By choosing to see the positive aspects in others, life takes on a radiant hue. This perspective becomes a guiding light, illuminating the path toward your goals. Embrace the transformative power of recognizing the inherent beauty around you, for in doing so, you will find the strength to step confidently toward the aspirations that shape your journey.

January 8: Embrace your amazing awesomeness.

On this day, acknowledge the incredible, awe-inspiring person you are both inside and out. Recognize your beauty and cultivate self-love. This reservoir of inner strength will serve as a guiding light, leading you confidently toward the attainment of your ultimate goals. Embrace your uniqueness, cherish the beauty within, and let self-love be the compass that directs your journey toward the culmination of your aspirations.

January 9: Celebrate your progress.

Take a moment today to be proud of the remarkable distance you've covered in this journey we call life. Acknowledge your achievements, both big and small. As you stand here, reflect on your resilience and keep pushing forward, for you are closer to your destination than you realize.

January 10: Stay focused and inspired.

Maintain your focus, keep your thoughts organized, and draw inspiration from what lies ahead. Look at the big picture of where you are headed, and let this broader perspective guide your actions. By staying committed and connected to your goals, you pave the way for a future filled with accomplishments.

January 13: Keep going, you've got this.

Don't give up; keep moving forward. If you decide to change course, it's not quitting—it's an evolution in how you approach your journey. You've got the strength and resilience to overcome challenges.

January 14: Find your heaven by stepping away from hell.

Sometimes, the only way to discover your personal heaven is to gracefully step back from the chaos of hell. Allow yourself the space to breathe, reflect, and find serenity amidst life's challenges.

January 15: Music as soul therapy.

Listen to the melody of life, as music serves as therapy for the soul. Choose tunes that uplift and inspire, devoid of politics, cursing, or explicit content. Let the pure sounds, like Metallica's "Unforgiven" or "Nothing Else Matters," fill your soul with positivity.

January 16: Live life your way.

This life is uniquely yours. Live it on your terms, following your path and embracing your individuality. Let no one else dictate how you shape your journey; it's yours to live authentically.

January 17: Cultivate positivity around you.

Work in a positive environment and surround yourself with like-minded individuals. The positivity they radiate will become a reflection in your own life.

January 18: Spread joy to feel joy.

Help others feel good, for in doing so, you cultivate a sense of joy within yourself. Making a positive impact on others is a reciprocal journey.

January 19: Immerse your mind in positivity.

Enforce positive thoughts into your mind and deflect all negativity. By consciously choosing optimism, you shape a mindset that propels you toward success.

January 20: Life is a party, act like it.

Embrace the party of life. Live, laugh, love, and keep moving toward your finish line. Celebrate the journey, finding joy in every step.

January 21: Be gentle with yourself.

Avoid being too hard on yourself. Follow your dreams and aspirations and fill your plate with activities that bring joy and fulfillment.

January 22: Be conscious, alive, and alert.

Be alive, be conscious in your life. Stay alert and be ready to rock this world on your unique journey through life. Continue to learn by feeding your curiosity and expanding your horizons by dedicating time to learning something new each day.

January 23: Stop and smell the roses.

Pause, appreciate, and savor the moments. Life is fleeting, and it's crucial not to lose sight of your purpose and what lights your flame. Take time at the end of the day to reflect on your experiences and express gratitude for the moments, big and small, that brought you joy or taught you something valuable.

January 24: Seize the present moment.

There isn't always a tomorrow. Take action now. Do what sparks your fire, pursue your desires, and don't miss out on what you're truly here for.

January 25: Hold the key to your life.

You possess the key to your life. Use it to unlock the multitude of possibilities waiting for you. As the Eagles sang, "So oftentimes it happens, we live our life in chains, and we never knew we have the key."

January 26: Embrace the challenge.

If something is easy, you might be doing it wrong. Challenges are essential to making sense of things and achieving meaningful outcomes.

January 27: Protect your sparkle.

Don't let anyone put dust on your sparkle. Believe in yourself and respect your worth, for no one else will do it for you. Take time to be grateful for this day. Allow yourself to spread kindness and positivity to those around you. Whether it is a compliment, a smile, or a small act of generosity, your actions can have a ripple effect on others' days.

January 28: Closer to success every day.

Celebrate the progress you make daily. You are reaching your goals and getting closer to success with each passing day.

January 29: Cultivate gratitude.

What are you grateful for? Write down ten things each day. This practice lifts and inspires, fostering a positive outlook that propels you forward.

January 30: Organize your life, one bed at a time.

Living an organized life starts with small steps. Begin by making your bed and establishing both evening and morning routines.

January 31: Let go and move forward.

This is the day to let go. Release fear, pain, comparisons, worries, guilt, judgment, anger, regrets, and blame. Letting go empowers you to move confidently toward your goals and aspirations.

FEBRUARY

A Journey through Affection

February 1: Write for self-discovery.

Today, focus on yourself. Just write. Pour out your thoughts, manifest your dreams, and pen an affirmation that resonates with your soul. Inspire and motivate yourself, cultivating a positive space that celebrates the unique essence of who you are.

February 2: Love yourself fully.

On this day, choose to love yourself unconditionally. Embrace each moment of this journey to the fullest, living in a way that aligns with the love and grace that God intends for you.

February 3: Stay resilient in storms.

Maintain your strength in the face of challenges. Don't let the rain hit you too hard and shield yourself from negativity. Remember, after every storm, the sun will shine again. You are strong.

February 4: Embrace imperfections.

You are not perfect, and that's perfectly okay. Embrace your imperfections, love yourself exactly as God made you, and celebrate the unique qualities that define who you are.

February 5: Trust your inner wisdom.

Listen to your inner wisdom and make great decisions today. You possess the strength and intuition to navigate this journey. Trust yourself; you've got this.

February 6: Spread joy and good vibes.

Infect the world with joy and good vibes today. Your positive energy has the power to uplift others and create a ripple effect of happiness.

February 7: Fail to learn.

Understand that failure is a part of the journey. Use each failure as a stepping stone to learning and growth. Embrace the lessons that come with every setback.

February 8: Embrace simplicity.

Follow the KISS theory (Keep It Simple, Stupid). Navigate straightforwardly and don't let anything obstruct your path. Embrace simplicity as a guiding principle and move forward with clarity and focus.

February 9: Prayer and positive practice.

Take time to pray today. As the Bible says, "What you ponder is what you are going to practice." Your thoughts shape your actions. Keep moving forward toward your finish line with positivity and purpose.

February 10: Change now, shape your future.

While we can't alter the past, we have the power to change our actions now. Start reshaping your path today, steering toward the ending you desire for your life story.

February 11: Take responsibility, be your best self.

Own your actions, acknowledge your feelings, and strive to be the best version of yourself. Taking responsibility is the first step toward personal growth.

February 12: Prayer for strength.

Devote today to prayer, seeking strength from God to effortlessly meet and achieve your goals.

February 13: Confront fear, don't fear fear.

Fear is often false evidence appearing real. Learn to manage and confront it. Don't let fear cripple you; reject the negative voices and move forward boldly.

February 14: Spread love, receive tenfold.

Show love today, not just because it's Valentine's Day, but because when you give love, it returns to you tenfold.

February 15: Love yourself, acknowledge your journey.

Today, express love to yourself. Acknowledge the fantastic job you're doing on your personal journey.

February 16: Simplify life, plan ahead.

Make life easier today. Lay out your outfit the night before, making your morning smoother for tomorrow.

February 17: Organize your space.

Take a step to organize one part of your house today. Avoid procrastination; tomorrow becomes tomorrow again. Take mindful breaks today. Pause and breathe throughout the day. Take time to recenter yourself. This could be as simple as a few deep breaths or a quick mindfulness exercise.

February 18: Face Life head-on, stay focused.

Confront life directly today. Remove distractions like alcohol that may divert your focus from your finish line.

February 19: Stay resilient, you're doing great.

Don't let anyone break you down. Recognize that you've got this, and you're doing a great job.

February 20: Value yourself, know your worth.

On this day, understand your value. Recognize that this journey is yours, and you are fully equipped to navigate it.

February 21: Conquer your demons, embrace your beauty.

We all have internal struggles. Don't let them in. You are beautiful, and you have the strength to face challenges on your own.

February 22: Music as therapy.

Utilize music for therapy. Let the lyrics uplift and guide you through your day.
Nourish your body with nutritious foods that provide sustained energy throughout the day. Opt for whole grain, fruits, vegetables, lean proteins, and plenty of water.

February 23: Believe in yourself.

Believe in the uniqueness that is you. You have the power to choose to stay or move forward.

February 24: Pursue your dreams, take chances.

Don't delay your dreams. Take a chance, for dreams are reachable, and nothing is impossible.

Connect with nature today. Spend time outdoors, even if it's just a few minutes in your backyard or nearby park. Nature has a calming effect on the mind and body, reducing stress and increasing feelings of well-being.

February 25: Act today, not tomorrow.

Seize the moment today, not tomorrow. Dive into organizing the chaos, get motivated, and let inspiration guide you to manifest your vision into reality.

February 26: Month-end reflection and readjustment.

As the month closes in fast, take a day to regroup. Reflect on each day of this month, ensuring you're on the right path toward the fulfillment your story desires.

February 27: Cleanse and organize.

Today, take out the metaphorical dirty laundry. Pull yourself together, organize your surroundings, tidy up your sock drawer, and align your ducks in a row for a fresh start.

February 28: Embrace gratitude today and get physical.

Let's get it started! Clean up, prepare, and get ready for a beautiful new month. Establish a nightly routine, take care of dental hygiene, wash your face, and lay out your outfit for the next day. Life won't wait, so get going and make each day count.

MARCH

Springing into Each Day, Embrace Renewal and Growth

March 1: March forward with purpose and determination.

Step into this month with a clear goal in mind. Take the necessary steps to lift yourself up. Keep a smile on your face and continue moving toward that goal line you're aiming for.

March 2: Embrace gratitude on this day.

Incorporate movement into your day, whether a brisk walk, yoga session, or simply taking the stairs instead of the elevator. Physical activity releases endorphins, boosting your mood and energy levels. This day is dedicated to gratitude. Walk into it with thankfulness at the forefront of your mind. Recognize and appreciate the positive aspects of your life.

March 3: Elevate your day by focusing on positivity and gratitude.

Take today to another level. Do something out of the ordinary, challenge yourself, and infuse a sense of excitement into your routine. Intentionally, incorporate activities like meditation, stretching, or journaling to set a positive tone for the day ahead.

March 4: Embrace discomfort for growth.

Step out of your comfort zone today. Embrace discomfort and do something that makes the uncomfortable feel okay. Growth often lies just beyond our comfort boundaries.

Feel free to provide the continuation for March 5 if you have specific ideas in mind!

March 5: Acceptance.

In the grand tapestry of life, there are threads we can weave, and there are threads beyond our control. Today, let us embark on a journey of acceptance, embracing the wisdom to distinguish between the two.

Acceptance does not imply resignation; rather, it empowers us to navigate the intricate dance between what we can change and what we cannot. It is the cornerstone of serenity, fostering a profound understanding of the beauty that lies in surrendering to the natural flow of existence.

March 6: Radiate your inner beauty.

On this day, let the mirror reflect not just an image but a declaration: you are beautiful, and you are worth it. Today is a celebration of your unique essence, a reminder to embrace the beauty that resides within and radiate it outward.

March 7: Embrace courage.

Today, let courage be your guiding star. You have within you the strength to face challenges, overcome obstacles, and embrace the possibilities that await. Your goal for today is simple yet profound: cultivate courage.

March 8: Embrace faith.

On this day, let faith be your anchor. Faith is not just a belief; it's a force that propels you forward, a guiding light in times of uncertainty. Your mantra for today is simple yet profound: have faith, for you've got this.

March 9: The continuation proceeded courageously.

Reflect on your courageous moments from the other day. Let courage be not just a fleeting visitor but a constant companion. Today is an invitation to make courage your friend and keep moving forward on this remarkable journey.

March 10: The magic of a smile

Today, let happiness be as simple as a smile. Turn that frown upside down, and watch the world transform around you. March 10 is a reminder that joy is within reach, and it starts with the curve of your lips.

March 11: Touching souls with kindness

Today is an opportunity to weave threads of positivity into the fabric of life. March 11 beckons you to reach out and touch someone's soul. In doing so, you not only make a difference in their day but also cultivate a warmth within yourself.

March 12: Shine bright like a diamond.

Today is a reminder to let your inner light shine with the brilliance of a diamond or the brightest star in the night sky. March 12 invites you to release the radiance within, allowing your unique glow to illuminate the world around you.

March 13: Cultivating inner peace

On this day, let the essence of inner peace be your guiding light. March 13 is an invitation to embrace tranquility within, recognizing that when you are at peace, your entire world functions with greater harmony and clarity.

March 14: The power of willpower

Today is a celebration of willpower—the driving force that propels us toward our aspirations. March 14 is a reminder that where there's a will, there's a way. Take a confident step in the direction of your dreams, and as you do, listen to the wisdom resonating from within.

March 15: Nurturing dreams

Today is a celebration of the belief that dreams do come true. March 15 invites you to embrace the power of manifestation by putting your dreams out into the universe. As you do, watch with anticipation as your dreams flourish and unfold in unexpected and beautiful ways.

March 16: Embrace self-belief and miracles.

Today, let the affirmation resonate within your core: to have miracles is to simply believe in oneself. March 16 is a celebration of the profound power that belief in your own capabilities holds—the catalyst for the extraordinary to manifest in your life.

March 17: Sparkle today and each day ahead.

Embrace the radiance within you and let it shine relentlessly, illuminating every corner of your existence. Believe fiercely in your ability to sparkle brighter with each passing day, for your inner light knows no bonds. Embrace the journey of self-discovery and self-love, knowing that your sparkle is unique and incomparable. Let it guide you through life's twists and turns, reminding you of the magic that resides within you. So stand tall, embrace your sparkle, and let it illuminate the world around you with its undeniable brilliance.

March 18: Choose positivity.

On this day, March 18, let the mantra resound in your heart: anything positive today is better than anything negative. Embrace the transformative power of positivity and consciously choose the path illuminated by optimism, gratitude, and joy.

March 19: Rediscover the wisdom within.

On this special day, March 19, take a moment to listen to your inner voice. Today, let the guidance of your inner child lead you on a journey of self-discovery, joy, and authenticity.

Listen to your inner voice in the symphony of daily life. Your inner voice is the melody that often goes unheard. March 19 invites you to pause, be still, and tune in to the whispers of your intuition. Your inner voice holds the wisdom and guidance you need to navigate challenges and embrace opportunities.

March 20: The power of positive thoughts

On this transformative day, March 20, immerse yourself in the understanding that positive thoughts are the seeds from which positive emotions and actions bloom. Today is an exploration of the profound connection between your mindset and the vibrant tapestry of your daily life.

March 21: The equation of performance

On this empowering day, March 21, delve into the understanding that actions are the building blocks of performance, and performance, in turn, shapes the entirety of your outcome. Today is a reminder that every intentional step you take contributes to the masterpiece of your life.

March 22: The power of motions and actions

On this pivotal day, March 22, immerse yourself in the recognition that every motion and action you undertake carries the potential to shape the trajectory of your day. Today, embrace the understanding that what you think or do has the power to make or break the essence of your experience. Motions and actions: architects of your day.

Your day is a canvas waiting to be painted with the brushstrokes of your motions and actions. March 22 encourages you to be mindful of the thoughts you entertain and the actions you take. These are the architects that construct the landscape of your day—a day that can be shaped by intention, purpose, and the choices you make.

March 23: The ripple of goodness

On this uplifting day, March 23, embrace a simple yet profound truth: do good, and good will come to you. Today, immerse yourself in the transformative power of kindness and witness how the ripples of goodness enhance the fabric of your day.

March 24: The language of action and words

On this contemplative day, March 24, delve into the profound truth that actions speak louder than words. Choose your words carefully, for they hold power, but let your actions be the eloquent expression of your intentions and values.

March 25: Embrace action, banish procrastination.

On this empowering day, March 25, cast aside the chains of procrastination and embrace the power of action. In the journey of life, there's no room for delay. Today, pull yourself up with determination, and let the mantra be: "Do, do, do."

No procrastinating: Seize the moment for March 25 is a call to action, a declaration that procrastination has no place in the narrative of your day. Seize the moment, for in each moment lies an opportunity to move forward, to make progress, and to contribute to the unfolding story of your life. Today is a canvas waiting for the strokes of your endeavors.

March 26: Empower yourself, move forward.

On this day of self-empowerment, March 26, recognize the profound truth: it's all you. No one else is going to save you from yourself today. Embrace the power within, and with unwavering determination, propel yourself forward.

March 27: Reap and you will get. You make the choices. Make it happen today.

On this empowering day, March 27, embrace the power of your choices. Just as you sow seeds, so shall you reap the harvest. Today, make intentional choices that align with your goals and aspirations. Your decisions shape the landscape of your journey, so seize the opportunity to plant seeds of growth, joy, and fulfillment. It's your time to make it happen.

March 28: It's all in how you look at it.

March 28 is a day of perspective. Life is a canvas, and the colors you choose to paint with are determined by your outlook. Today, embrace the understanding that it's all in how you look at it. Choose optimism, find beauty in simplicity, and let gratitude be your lens. As you shift your perspective, you'll discover the richness that lies in every moment.

March 29: Today, make a practical choice to grow.

On this day of growth, March 29, make practical choices that propel you forward. Every decision, no matter how small, has the potential to contribute to your personal and professional development. Identify areas for growth, set realistic goals, and take practical steps toward them. Today, let your choices become the stepping stones that lead to a stronger, wiser, and more fulfilled you.

March 30: Shine or be dull, you choose.

March 30 is a day to embrace your radiance. You hold the power to shine brightly or remain dull, and today is a reminder to choose radiance. Let your unique qualities and strengths illuminate your path. Embrace positivity, share your light with others, and watch as your brilliance transforms not only your day but also the world around you. Today, choose to shine.

March 31: Ask and you will receive.

On this day of possibility, March 31, embrace the power of asking. Whether for guidance, support, or opportunities, recognize that asking is a declaration of your aspirations. Today, be bold in seeking what you need. Ask with confidence and open yourself to the abundance that awaits. Trust that as you seek, you shall find, and as you ask, you will receive.

APRIL

Blossoming Amidst Showers, Embracing Growth and Joy

April 1: Don't be fooled today.

On this playful day, April 1, navigate with discernment. While the world may play tricks, trust your instincts and move forward with a clear perspective. Approach situations with a balance of humor and wisdom, ensuring that your path remains steadfast even in the face of illusions.

April 2: Look at this beautiful new month as a time to change your mindset.

In the canvas of April 2, embrace the opportunity for a mental reset. View this beautiful new month as a blank slate for your thoughts. Choose positivity, set empowering intentions, and let your mindset bloom with the vibrant possibilities that this fresh start brings.

April 3: Begin working on yourself from the inside out; look in the mirror.

On April 3, initiate a journey of self-improvement. Start from within and gaze into the mirror—both literally and metaphorically. Reflect on your strengths and areas for growth. As you work on yourself from the inside out, embrace the transformative power of self-awareness and self-love.

April 4: Don't be shy; put yourself out there and look on the bright side.

In the spirit of April 4, step boldly into the spotlight. Don't be shy about showcasing your talents, ideas, or true self. Look on the bright side of situations, highlighting the positive aspects. As you put yourself out there, radiate confidence and optimism, inviting a cascade of positive energy into your endeavors.

April 5: What are you most proud of about yourself? Ask yourself.

On this introspective day, April 5, turn your attention inward. Take a moment to reflect on your journey and ask yourself, "What am I most proud of about myself?" Acknowledge your achievements, growth, and strengths. Celebrate the unique qualities that make you proud of the person you are.

April 6: Be confident today.

In the spirit of April 6, exude confidence in all that you do. Stand tall, believe in your abilities, and let your self-assured demeanor guide your actions. Confidence is a powerful force that not only influences how others perceive you but also shapes your own perception of what you can achieve. Today, carry yourself with confidence and embrace the strength that it brings.

April 7: Bring your light of joy wherever you go today. Illuminate everything in your path.

On this radiant day, April 7, become a beacon of joy. Let your positive energy shine and brighten the world around you. Wherever you go, bring the light of your spirit, illuminating the path for yourself and others.

April 8: Lead the way to a happy life today.

In the spirit of April 8, take on the role of a guide to happiness. Lead by example and infuse joy into your actions. Share smiles, encourage positivity, and inspire others to embark on a path that leads to a life filled with happiness.

April 9: Have love for all you see and touch today. No hatred, only love and positivity.

On this day of compassion, April 9, envelop everything with love. Cultivate a heart full of love for all you encounter. Let go of negativity and hatred, allowing only love and positivity to flow through your interactions and touch the lives of those around you.

April 10: Motivate yourself by adopting a selfless mindset while understanding your own self-worth.

Today, commit to the team, recognizing that collective effort can propel everyone forward. Expect challenges and pushbacks; they are part of the journey. When faced with resistance, approach it with empathy and a willingness to collaborate.

April 11: In pursuit of shared goals, unity becomes the driving force.

Working together to achieve a common objective not only multiplies efforts but also strengthens the bonds within the team. Each person brings a unique set of skills and perspectives; combining them fosters a dynamic and resilient group.

April 12: Understanding that anger can disrupt the harmony necessary for organized living is crucial.

Instead of allowing frustration to dominate, channel that energy into finding constructive solutions. An organized life isn't just about neat spaces; it extends to the clarity and order within our minds.

Consider the ultimate goal—organized living. This doesn't merely imply a tidy environment but encompasses a harmonious existence where tasks are streamlined, and relationships are nurtured. By alleviating unnecessary anxiety, we create room for growth, joy, and meaningful connections.

April 13: Inspiration is the magic that transforms routine into remarkable.

Find sources of inspiration around you—a meaningful quote, a piece of art, or the beauty of nature. Let these moments infuse your day with creativity and purpose.

April 14: Goals

Today is about you, your goals, and the journey toward them. Take a moment to visualize the success you're striving for. Envision the path ahead, and with each step, feel your radiance intensify.

April 15: Inspire others.

As you navigate this day, let your light inspire others. Encourage those around you to embrace their uniqueness and pursue their aspirations. In doing so, you create a constellation of shared dreams, each star contributing to the brilliance of the whole.

April 16: You will go a long way in this journey on your path with your positive light as long as you follow the bright path.

On this luminous day, April 16, trust in the power of your positive light. Follow the bright path before you, and let optimism guide your journey. Your positivity will illuminate the way, leading you to remarkable destinations on your path.

April 17: A day to not be regretful of anything. This is all a learning experience here on earth.

In the spirit of April 17, release regrets. Recognize that every experience is a valuable lesson on this earthly journey. Embrace the wisdom gained from challenges and triumphs alike, understanding that each moment contributes to your growth and understanding.

April 18: Aspire today to make a special day an excellent day of performance.

On April 18, set your aspirations high. Aim for excellence in every endeavor. Whether big or small, approach each task with the intention to perform at your best. Today is an opportunity to turn the ordinary into the extraordinary through your dedication and effort.

April 19: Do not be resentful; it will cause you illness.

In the light of April 19, release resentment. Recognize its detrimental impact on your well-being. Choose to let go, forgive, and cultivate a heart free from bitterness. By embracing positivity and understanding, you foster a healthier and happier life.

April 20: Be you today; worry about you today and see how the world around you changes.

On this empowering day, April 20, prioritize self-care. Focus on being authentic to yourself and your needs. As you nurture your well-being, observe how the world around you transforms in response to the positive energy you radiate.

April 21: Make every moment a fresh new start. The beginning can be started at any time.

In the spirit of April 21, recognize the power of renewal. Approach each moment with a fresh perspective, allowing the potential for new beginnings at any time. Every choice is an opportunity to start anew, shaping your journey with intention and positivity.

April 22: On this day, surround yourself with positive, better people than yourself. Individuals that you can benefit from and not bring you down.

In the embrace of April 22, curate your surroundings with positivity. Seek the company of individuals who uplift and inspire you. Surround yourself with people whose energy elevates yours, fostering an environment where growth, support, and mutual benefit flourish. Today, choose connections that contribute to your well-being and aspirations.

April 23: Have peace of mind that this is all about you. You plant the seed and watch it grow. You plant whatever you want to grow in your field.

On this empowering day, April 23, find solace in the knowledge that your journey is uniquely yours. You hold the power to plant the seeds of your aspirations. Choose the seeds wisely, nurture them with intention, and watch as your efforts cultivate the growth of what you desire in the field of your life. Today, embrace the agency you have in shaping your own path.

April 24: Do not be the smartest person in the room today. Wherever the day will lead you, find out something new. Always be ready to learn from someone.

On this enriching day, April 24, embrace the spirit of humility and curiosity. Rather than being the smartest, be open to learning from others. Seek out opportunities to discover something new wherever your journey takes you. Approach each interaction with a willingness to absorb knowledge and insights from those around you. Today, let the joy of continuous learning guide your path.

April 25: Dream and visualize, and it will soon come true. This is your party. You are the planner of your event here on your journey.

On this visionary day, April 25, let your dreams take flight. Envision the possibilities and embrace the role of the planner in the grand event of your life journey. Your dreams are invitations to a magnificent celebration; the more vividly you visualize, the more likely they are to manifest. Today, revel in the creative power of your dreams and set the stage for the extraordinary.

April 26: Troubles will come, but you have the power to make them go.

On this resilient day, April 26, recognize your inner strength. While troubles may visit, you hold the power to overcome and make them fade away. Face challenges with courage, resilience, and the unwavering belief that you have the capability to navigate through any storm.

April 27: Shine like a rockstar. You are the only shooting star in this universe; there is no other.

In the celestial light of April 27, embrace your unique brilliance. You are a rare and shining star in the vast universe. Let your radiance illuminate the world around you. Shine with the confidence and allure of a rock star, for there is no other star quite like you. Today, let your light dazzle and inspire.

April 28: The whole world will shine bright to you as soon as you show your light.

On this illuminating day, April 28, recognize the power of your own light. When you share your unique brilliance, the world around you responds in kind. Today, let your light shine brightly, and watch as the entire world reflects that radiance back to you.

April 29: As this month unfolds, from your positiveness and courage, let's close it on a good note.

In the spirit of April 29, carry forward the positivity and courage that has defined this month. As the days unfold, leave a positive imprint on each moment. Approach challenges with resilience, and let the closing notes of this month resonate with accomplishment, growth, and joy.

April 30: Organize something that is making you anxious, and let's end this month on a good note.

On this concluding day of the month, April 30, embark on a mission of organization. Tackle the source of anxiety and bring order to chaos. By resolving what makes you uneasy, you set the stage for a harmonious conclusion to the month, leaving you with a sense of accomplishment and peace.

MAY

May Joy Blossom Embracing the Gifts of the Season

May 1: In moments of doubt, remember that your strength surpasses your perceived limitations.

Challenges may test you, but they also unveil your capacity for growth. Embrace adversity as an opportunity to showcase the unwavering power within your spirit.

As you navigate this day, keep pushing forward toward your aspirations. Every step, no matter how small, is a testament to your determination. Life's path may be winding, but with each stride, you carve a trail of triumph, leaving behind footprints of resilience.

Acknowledge your achievements, both big and small. Celebrate the milestones on your journey, for they are the markers of your strength in action. Even in moments of uncertainty, your ability to persevere shines through, lighting the way for your continued progress.

May 2: Surround yourself with positivity and affirmations.

Remind yourself daily of your capabilities and the goals you're working toward. Your mindset is a powerful tool; wield it with intention and let it propel you forward, clearing the obstacles in your path.

Life's twists and turns are inevitable, but so is your strength. Embrace the challenges with the knowledge that you have the fortitude to overcome them. The journey toward what you want in life is a testament to your resilience, determination, and the strength that resides within you.

Today, affirm your inner power, keep pushing forward, and remember, you are stronger than you think.

May 3: If you prepare from the night before, believe me, you will have a better tomorrow. For example, lay your outfit out and do a nightly routine.

On this insightful day, May 3, recognize the power of preparation. Set the stage for a better tomorrow by organizing and preparing the night before. Lay out your outfit, establish a nightly routine, and create a foundation that ensures a smoother, more intentional start to the day ahead. Today, invest in the peace and productivity that thoughtful preparation can bring.

May 4: May the fourth be with you. Push the demons away and make room for vibrance and beauty today.

On this whimsical day, May 4, channel the force within you to overcome challenges. Push away any negative forces or inner demons that may cloud your path. Create space for vibrance and beauty to flourish, allowing the light of positivity to guide your journey. May the fourth be with you as you navigate toward a day filled with resilience and brilliance.

May 5: Morning routine leads to a nightly routine, which leads to a well-organized life.

On this mindful day, May 5, recognize the symbiotic relationship between your morning and nightly routines. As you establish intentional habits at both ends of the day, you pave the way for a well-organized and balanced life. Embrace the rhythm of routine, allowing it to bring structure, productivity, and harmony to your daily journey.

May 6: You only need you in this journey. Anyone who is taking up space that you do not approve of will have to wait. No one else will be there but you.

On this empowering day, May 6, reclaim your space and journey. Acknowledge the significance of your presence and set boundaries for your well-being. If someone doesn't align with your journey or values, let them wait outside your sacred space. Today, prioritize your own path, embracing the solitude and strength that comes from being true to yourself.

May 7: Kiss theory. Keep things simple in your day, your journey called life. Do not overthink them; keep them easy.

On this day of simplicity, May 7, embrace the KISS principle—Keep It Simple, Stupid. Navigate your journey with ease by avoiding unnecessary complexity. Simplify your day, your decisions, and your path, finding beauty in the straightforward and allowing simplicity to guide you toward clarity and peace.

May 8: You got this today. I am proud of you and how far you have come.

On this affirming day, May 8, acknowledge your resilience and progress. You've got the strength to face whatever comes your way. Take pride in your journey and remember how far you've come. Today is a testament to your capabilities.

May 9: You choose your battles in life. Do not fight if you do not have to.

In the spirit of May 9, exercise discernment. Pick your battles wisely, understanding that not every challenge requires your energy. Conserve your strength for the battles that truly matter, fostering a sense of balance and wisdom in your journey.

May 10: Be diligent today.

On this day of diligence, May 10, approach your tasks with focus and determination. Persevere through challenges, and let your diligence pave the way for achievement. Your commitment to excellence will contribute to your success and growth.

May 11: Peace for today and all the rest of your days here.

In the tranquility of May 11, cultivate a sense of peace. Let it envelop your day and become a constant companion on your journey. Seek moments of calmness, and allow peace to guide your thoughts, actions, and interactions.

May 12: Reach out to someone that you have not talked to in a while. Let them know you are thinking of them; you never know, they may be of help to you.

On this day of connection, May 12, foster relationships. Reach out to someone from your past, expressing your thoughts and appreciation. You never know what positive impact this connection may have, both for them and for you.

May 13: Look at people as helpers, not hurters.

In the spirit of May 13, shift your perspective. See others as potential allies and helpers rather than adversaries. Embrace a mindset of collaboration and support, fostering positive connections in your personal and professional interactions.

May 14: This is a special day. You are blessed, and many blessings are coming your way. Just keep believing.

On this day of gratitude, May 14, recognize the blessings that surround you. Believe in the abundance that is on its way. Your positive outlook and belief in yourself are powerful forces that attract goodness. Today is special, and so are you.

May 15: Put what you want out into the world today. Say it and see it happen. Believe it. Live it. Own it.

On this day of manifestation, May 15, speak your desires into the universe. Express what you want, visualize it with belief, and witness the power of your intentions. Live with confidence, embracing the journey of bringing your aspirations to life. Today, own the power of your words and watch as they shape the reality you wish to create.

May 16: Be organized, be positive, be ready to do great things.

On this day of readiness, May 16, set the tone for greatness. Embrace organization to streamline your efforts, cultivate positivity to fuel your spirit, and stand ready to embark on the journey of achieving great things. Today, your preparedness paves the way for success and fulfillment.

May 17: As the middle of the month starts to go into the end of the month, this does not mean any doors are closing in on you. It is opening for you to make and continue to make new and good things.

On this transitional day, May 17, recognize that the passage of time brings opportunities for new beginnings. The closing of one chapter signals the opening of another. Embrace the possibilities that lie ahead and continue to create and shape the narrative of your journey with optimism and purpose. The end of the month is not an ending but a gateway to fresh and promising experiences.

May 18: Today, enjoy a clear and uncluttered space. Find something to organize in your home that has been bothering you.

On this day of order, May 18, embrace the serenity of an organized environment. Tackle a task that has been lingering and create a clear and uncluttered space in your home. The harmony you cultivate externally will resonate internally.

May 19: Be a team leader, not a follower, in your own book of life. You make the pathway through your journey. Only you know where the road ends.

In the spirit of May 19, take charge of your narrative. Be the leader of your journey, paving your own path. You hold the pen to your story, and, as the main character, guide your narrative with intention, creating a journey uniquely yours.

May 20: This is your story. You are the main character. Today, show that in your story, you will make the right choices and be positive.

On this day of authorship, May 20, recognize the power you hold in crafting your own narrative. Make conscious choices and infuse positivity into your story. Today, exemplify the strength and resilience of the main character, that is, you.

May 21: Be in control of yourself today. Make good choices.

On this day of self-control, May 21, steer the course of your actions with intention. Make choices that align with your values and aspirations. By being in control of yourself, you shape the direction of your journey.

May 22: You are worthy. You are good enough. Have good energy. Believe you are worth it and love yourself today.

On this day of self-love, May 22, affirm your worthiness. Radiate positive energy and embrace the truth that you are good enough. Believe in your inherent value and shower yourself with love and appreciation throughout the day.

May 23: Make progress today by getting rid of three items at least or pieces of clutter that do not serve a purpose.

On this day of decluttering, May 23, take proactive steps toward progress. Identify three items or pieces of clutter that no longer serve a purpose in your life and let them go. Create space for new energy and opportunities by clearing away what is no longer needed. Today, embrace the liberating feeling of simplifying your surroundings.

May 24: Keep focus on the prize. You are here to become whatever you want in this world. Keep focused, and you will reach the pinnacle.

On this day of determination, May 24, fix your gaze on your goals. You have the power to become whatever you desire in this world. Stay focused on your aspirations, and you'll steadily move closer to realizing your dreams.

May 25: Everything has a place. Put things in your life in order. When things are in order, you feel better.

In the spirit of May 25, embrace orderliness. Assign a place for everything in your life, creating a harmonious and organized environment. Witness the positive impact it has on your well-being as you navigate through each day.

May 26: Your thoughts are calm today. Your surroundings are organized. Keep calm and neat and move forward in this journey.

On this day of tranquility, May 26, cultivate a calm mind and organized surroundings. The synergy between peaceful thoughts and an ordered environment propels you forward with clarity and purpose. Keep calm, stay neat, and advance confidently on your journey.

May 27: Today will be successful. Make good choices, and success will come easily to you.

In the spirit of May 27, envision success. Make mindful choices aligned with your goals, and success will naturally flow into your life. Today, seize the opportunities that come your way with confidence and intention.

May 28: Today, you will be confident. Know what you want and go for it.

On this day of confidence, May 28, stand tall in your aspirations. Know what you want, and boldly pursue it. Your confidence is a powerful force that propels you toward success. Embrace the self-assurance within you and move forward with purpose.

May 29: You are strong. This makes you great and helps you keep moving toward your goals and the finish line.

On this empowering day, May 29, recognize the strength within you. Your resilience and fortitude contribute to your greatness. Keep moving forward, propelled by the power of your strength, and journey confidently toward your goals and the finish line of success.

May 30: As this month comes to an end, it is not the end for you to do great things.

On this concluding day of May, recognize that the end of the month is not a conclusion but a transition. Embrace the opportunities that continue to unfold. The journey of doing great things extends beyond the calendar, and you are well-equipped for the chapters that lie ahead.

May 31: You are an unstoppable force of nature. Keep following your natural gut instinct, and all will be bright for your day.

On this day of resilience, May 31, tap into your unstoppable nature. Trust your instincts, for they are your compass. As you follow your innate guidance, you become a force that propels you toward brightness and success. Today, let your instincts guide you to a day filled with positivity and accomplishment.

JUNE

Preparing for Radiance and Welcoming the Summer Sun

June 1: The ripple effect of positive actions

Positive thoughts are not isolated; they set in motion a ripple effect that extends beyond your internal landscape. June invites you to be aware of how your positive thoughts influence your actions. When your mindset is one of possibility and optimism, your actions naturally align with the energy of positivity, creating a ripple of constructive impact.

June 2: Embrace the momentum of positivity.

Positive thoughts, emotions, and actions create a harmonious flow of momentum. June 2 is a day to recognize that, just as a stream gains strength as it flows, the momentum of positivity builds in your life. Embrace this momentum, and let it guide you toward experiences that resonate with joy, kindness, and fulfillment.

June 3: Cultivate a positive mindset.

In the face of challenges, June 3 encourages you to consciously cultivate a positive mindset. Choose to see solutions rather than problems, opportunities rather than obstacles. Your thoughts are the paintbrush, and your life is the canvas—create a masterpiece filled with vivid strokes of positivity.

June 4: May your day blossom with positivity.

On this day, let your day blossom with the beauty of positive thoughts. As you nurture an optimistic mindset, observe how it transforms your emotions and influences your actions. Your journey is an ever-evolving canvas, and today, let positivity be the vibrant palette that paints a life rich in joy, kindness, and fulfillment.

Actions: The foundation of performance
Your journey is sculpted by the actions you choose to take. This day encourages you to be mindful of the decisions, efforts, and intentions that define your path. Your actions are the foundation upon which the structure of your performance is built—a series of intentional steps that shape the narrative of your life.

June 5: Performance: a reflection of actions

Performance is not just an outcome; it's a reflection of the cumulative effect of your actions. June 5 invites you to view performance as a mirror that echoes the consistency, dedication, and quality of your efforts. How you perform in various aspects of your life is a testament to the actions you consistently bring into play.

Affirmation: My actions shape my performance; affirm to yourself on this day, "My actions shape my performance, and my performance influences my entire outcome. Today, I choose intentional actions that contribute to a performance aligned with my aspirations and values."

June 6: Strive for excellence in every action.

As you embark on this day, strive for excellence in every action you undertake. Whether it's a small task or a significant endeavor, let each action be infused with purpose, diligence, and a commitment to excellence. Your performance is elevated when fueled by the intention to bring your best self into every moment.

June 7: Consistency is key to performance.

Consistency is the silent architect of performance. June 7 emphasizes the importance of regular, intentional actions. It's the daily commitment, the small steps taken consistently, that weave together to create a performance that stands the test of time and builds the foundation for your overall outcome.

June 8: Reflect on your performance.

Take moments throughout the day to reflect on your performance. This day is an opportunity for introspection. Ask yourself: how have my actions contributed to my performance? What adjustments can I make to align my actions more closely with my goals? Through reflection, you gain insights that empower you to refine and enhance your performance.

June 9: May your outcome reflect your best performance.

On this day, may the equation of actions, performance, and outcome guide you toward the realization of your aspirations. Recognize the power you hold in the choices you make and the actions you take. As you bring intentionality and excellence into your performance, may your overall outcome reflect the masterpiece that arises from the brushstrokes of your daily efforts. Today, embrace the transformative journey of turning intentional actions into a performance that shapes the essence of your life.

June 10: What you think: the prelude to action

Your thoughts are the prelude to action. Today invites you to observe the quality of your thoughts. Are they uplifting, empowering, and aligned with your goals? Your thoughts set the stage for the actions that follow, creating a harmonious symphony or discordant notes in the melody of your day.

Affirmation: My thoughts and actions shape my day, and affirm to yourself today, "My thoughts and actions shape my day. Today, I choose thoughts that empower me, and I take actions aligned with my aspirations. I am the architect of my experience, and I am intentional in creating a day filled with purpose and positivity."

June 11: Make or break: the impact of your choices

What you think or do today holds the potential to make or break the essence of your day. Today emphasizes the profound impact of your choices. Choose thoughts that uplift and actions that propel you forward. In doing so, you set the stage for a day filled with productivity, positivity, and fulfillment.

June 12: Conscious decision-making

As you navigate through this day, be a conscious decision-maker. Today is an invitation to pause and consider the consequences of your thoughts and actions. By approaching each moment with intentionality, you ensure that your day unfolds in alignment with your values and aspirations.

June 13: May your day be shaped by positive intentions.

On this day, let the awareness of the power of your motions and actions guide you. What you think or do today is a brushstroke on the canvas of your day. May your thoughts be positive, your actions intentional, and your day be shaped by the masterpiece of your conscious choices. Today, be the artist of your experience, creating a day that resonates with purpose, joy, and fulfillment.

Affirmation: My actions create ripples of goodness. Affirm to yourself today, "My actions create ripples of goodness. Today, I choose to do good, knowing that kindness, compassion, and positivity will find their way back to me. I am a source of goodness in the world."

June 14: The joy of giving and receiving

Engage in acts of kindness not with the expectation of receiving but with the joy of giving. June 14 is an opportunity to experience the fulfillment that comes from making a positive impact on someone else's day. By radiating kindness, you become a conduit for the reciprocal flow of goodness.

June 15: Small acts, big impact

The magic of doing good often lies in the small, heartfelt gestures. Today encourages you to seize moments to make a difference, whether through a kind word, a helping hand, or a thoughtful gesture. These small acts have the potential to create significant positive impacts on both yourself and those around you.

Reflect on the goodness. Take moments to reflect on the goodness you've shared throughout the day. June 15 is a day of mindfulness, inviting you to observe how your actions have created ripples of positivity. Acknowledge the joy that comes from contributing to the well-being of others.

June 16: May your day be filled with goodness.

On this day, let the goodness you sow be the guiding force of your day. As you engage in acts of kindness, observe how the positive energy reverberates, creating a tapestry of joy, connection, and fulfillment. Today, be a beacon of goodness, and allow the beauty of your actions to return to you in unexpected and wonderful ways.

June 17: Do good: planting seeds of positivity.

Today is an invitation to be a bearer of goodness. Choose kindness, generosity, and compassion as your companions for the day. Every act of kindness is a seed planted, and as you sow them throughout your day, you contribute to a garden of positivity that blooms with the potential for joy, connection, and fulfillment.

Goodness begets goodness. The beauty of doing good lies in its reciprocal nature. June 17 encourages you to recognize that the positive energy you extend to others has a way of returning to you. Whether through the smile of a stranger, a gesture of gratitude, or unexpected kindness, goodness begets goodness, creating a harmonious cycle of positive interactions.

June 18: Actions: a powerful expression

Today invites you to recognize the potency of actions as a language in itself. Your actions convey sincerity, commitment, and authenticity in ways that words alone cannot. In the symphony of life, your actions become the melody that resonates with impact and influence.

June 19: Words: choose them thoughtfully.

While words have their place, June 19 encourages you to choose them thoughtfully. The words you speak have the ability to inspire, uplift, or create understanding. Yet be mindful that words can also be fleeting. It is through consistent and aligned actions that the true essence of your intentions is revealed.

Affirmation: My actions align with my words. Affirm to yourself on June 19, "My actions speak volumes, and my words are chosen carefully. Today, I align my actions with my words, creating a harmonious expression of my intentions. I recognize the power in both and use them consciously to shape my interactions and relationships."

June 20: Consistency in expression

The power of your communication lies in the consistency between your words and actions. June 20 is an opportunity to ensure that your actions echo the promises, values, and sentiments you convey through words. Let your actions be the living testament to the principles you hold dear.

June 21: Integrity in communication

Integrity is the bridge between words and actions. Today calls for a commitment to integrity in your communication. When your actions align with your words, you build a foundation of trust and authenticity. This, in turn, strengthens your connections and relationships.

June 22: Lead by example.

In your personal and professional life, lead by example. Today encourages you to embody the qualities and values you speak about. Let your actions be a guiding light for others, inspiring them to not only hear your words but witness the sincerity in your deeds.

June 23: May your actions resonate with authenticity.

On June 23, let the language of your actions resonate with authenticity. Choose your words carefully and ensure that they are backed by the strength and sincerity of your deeds. As you navigate through the day, may your actions become a powerful expression of your character, values, and intentions. Today, let your actions speak with a clarity that surpasses the limitations of words alone.

June 24: Pull yourself up: a gesture of empowerment.

When faced with tasks or challenges, pull yourself up with a spirit of empowerment. June 24 invites you to rise above inertia, self-doubt, or hesitation. Be your own source of motivation and let the act of pulling yourself up be a symbol of your commitment to taking charge of your journey.

Affirmation: Today, I am an agent of action. Affirm to yourself on June 24, "Today, I am an agent of action. I banish procrastination and embrace the power of 'do, do, do.' I pull myself up with determination, recognizing that every action I take propels me forward on my path of growth and accomplishment."

June 25: Embrace the momentum of doing.

The momentum of accomplishment is built through action. June 25 encourages you to embrace the rhythm of doing. Break down tasks into manageable steps, prioritize, and take deliberate actions. As you do, you set in motion a dynamic energy that propels you closer to your goals.

June 26: Overcome resistance with action.

Resistance often melts away in the face of action. June 25 is an invitation to overcome inertia or resistance by immersing yourself in the doing. As you tackle tasks and pursue your objectives, you'll find that the act of doing itself becomes a catalyst for motivation and progress.

June 27: Celebrate every "day" as if it were your final one.

Celebrate every "day" as a victory. June 27 is not just about completing major tasks; it's about recognizing the significance of every step forward. By acknowledging and celebrating your actions, you create a positive cycle of motivation and accomplishment.

June 28: May your day be filled with productivity "dos."

On June 28, let the echoes of "do, do, do" resonate throughout your day. Banish procrastination, pull yourself up with determination, and embrace the satisfaction that comes from taking intentional actions. May your day be filled with productive "dos" that contribute to the realization of your goals and the shaping of a purposeful journey.

June 29: Have inspiration today that all things are possible. When one door shuts, another soon opens.

Embrace the boundless possibilities that June 29 holds. Today, let inspiration be your guiding light, and remember that even when one door closes, another awaits your discovery. Life is a tapestry of opportunities; trust in the journey and welcome the doors of possibility that open before you.

June 30: A house can be organized. It takes time to create a mess. It will take time to get things in order.

In the canvas of your space, June 30 whispers the wisdom that organization is a journey, not a destination. Just as it takes time to create a mess, allow patience to guide you in restoring order. One step at a time, one corner at a time, and soon, your house will reflect the clarity and peace you envision.

JULY

A Positive Summer Vibe Embracing the Joys of the Summer Season

July 1: It's all you: harness your power.

Today is a reminder that the key to your progress and well-being lies within yourself. It's all your choices, your actions, and your resilience. Today, harness the power within and take responsibility for steering the course of your day and, ultimately, your life towards your desired destination.

July 2: No one else will save you: be your own hero.

In the narrative of your life, be the hero of your own story. July 2 invites you to understand that relying on others to save you from challenges or obstacles is a fleeting hope. Instead, empower yourself to face adversity head-on, knowing that you possess the strength and resilience to overcome.

July 3: Affirmation: I am the architect of my destiny.

Affirm to yourself on July 3, "I am the architect of my destiny. Today, I recognize that it's all me. No one else is going to save me from myself, and that's empowering. I take charge, move forward with determination, and shape the path of my own journey."

July 4: Find independence today.

On this day of celebration, July 4, seek a different kind of independence. Free yourself from limiting beliefs, break the chains of self-doubt, and declare your independence from anything that holds you back. Embrace the freedom to be your authentic self, pursue your passions, and soar toward the limitless possibilities that await. Today, find the independence that empowers you to live life on your own terms.

July 5: Move forward: take purposeful steps.

Embrace the momentum of progress. July 5 encourages you to move forward with purposeful steps. Identify your goals, break them down into actionable tasks, and take each step with intention. As you move forward, you are actively creating the future you envision.

July 6: Face challenges head-on.

Challenges are inevitable, but so is your ability to face them. July 6 is a call to confront challenges with courage. Whether big or small, view each challenge as an opportunity to grow stronger and more resilient. Your ability to navigate challenges is a testament to your inner strength.

July 7: Embrace self-reliance.

Self-reliance is a powerful ally on your journey. July 7 celebrates the strength that comes from relying on yourself. Seek solutions within, trust your instincts, and believe in your capabilities. As you embrace self-reliance, you become the captain of your own ship, navigating the seas of life with purpose.

July 8: May your self-empowerment propel you forward.

On July 8, let the realization that "it's all you" be a source of empowerment. No one else is going to save you from yourself today, but that's where your strength lies. Take charge, move forward with determination, and let the unwavering power within you propel you toward the fulfillment of your aspirations. Today, embrace the role of the architect of your own destiny.

July 9: Accept what you cannot change.

Life, with its unpredictable twists and turns, often presents us with situations beyond our influence. These are the moments when acceptance becomes a transformative force. It doesn't mean giving up; instead, it encourages us to release the grip of resistance and find solace in the notion that not everything is within our command.

Accepting what you cannot change is an act of liberation. It frees the mind from the burden of futile resistance, allowing us to redirect our energy toward aspects of life where we can make a difference. As we embrace this acceptance, we find peace in the midst of chaos and resilience in the face of adversity.

July 10: Accept what you can control.

On the flip side, acceptance extends its benevolent touch to the realm of control. It urges us to recognize the areas where we hold sway, encouraging a sense of responsibility and agency. By acknowledging our power to shape certain aspects of our lives, we embark on a journey of intentional living.

Make today about consciously embracing the elements within your control. Whether it's the choices you make, the attitudes you adopt, or the actions you take, let acceptance guide you toward a harmonious alignment with your true self. The strength of acceptance lies not only in acknowledging what you can control but in leveraging that power to sculpt a life aligned with your aspirations.

July 11: Have the courage that you can do this.

In the tapestry of life, courage is the thread that stitches dreams into reality.

Acknowledge your fears and uncertainties but let them not define your journey. Have the courage to believe in yourself, in your abilities, and in the resilience that resides within.

Courage is not the absence of fear but the triumph over it. Recognize that every step you take, every challenge you confront, is an opportunity to showcase the courageous spirit that resides within you. Today is not about the absence of obstacles but about your ability to navigate them with unwavering courage.

July 12: You can do this.

Believe in your capabilities. You have overcome challenges before, and you possess the strength to triumph over the challenges of today. Trust in your skills, your intuition, and your capacity to learn and adapt. Today's goal is not just to face the day; it's to approach it with the conviction that you can handle whatever comes your way.

Embrace the challenges, for they are stepping stones toward growth and self-discovery. Each obstacle is an opportunity to showcase the courage that resides within your heart. You can do this, not just because you've done it before but because you are continually evolving, gaining wisdom, and becoming a stronger version of yourself.

July 13: Today, make it about acceptance.

As the sun rises on this day, let acceptance be your guiding star. Embrace the present moment, with all its uncertainties and certainties, as a gift to be treasured. In the tapestry of life, threads of acceptance weave a story of resilience, wisdom, and inner peace.

July 13 is a reminder that in acceptance, we find the key to unlocking the fullness of life. Accept what you cannot change, empower what you can control, and make today a celebration of the serenity that comes with embracing life in all its beautiful complexity.

July 14: You are beautiful.

Beauty is not a set of predefined standards but a kaleidoscope of individuality. Your quirks, imperfections, and uniqueness compose a symphony that is exclusively yours. Take a moment today to appreciate the beauty in your laughter, the sparkle in your eyes, and the strength in your spirit. You are a masterpiece, a work of art unfolding with each passing day.

July 15: You are worth it.

In a world that sometimes demands conformity, remember that your worth transcends external validations. Your value is innate, an intrinsic part of your being. Acknowledge your worthiness not as a result of achievements or comparisons but as a fundamental truth. You deserve love, joy, and fulfillment. Today, affirm your worthiness with each step you take.

July 16: Let your appearance light your way.

Your appearance is a canvas, and today is an opportunity to paint it with the hues of self-love and confidence. Choose attire that resonates with your spirit, wear colors that uplift your mood, and adorn yourself with elements that reflect your personality. Let your appearance be a mirror that reflects the beauty within, lighting your way on the fabulous path that lies ahead.

July 17: See your fabulous path.

As you step out into the world today, envision your path as a magnificent journey filled with opportunities, growth, and triumphs. Your appearance becomes not just a reflection but a projection of the confidence and determination that propel you forward. Embrace the fabulousness within you, for it is the beacon that illuminates the extraordinary path you tread.

Where you are headed and your path is not just a destination; it's a continuous evolution. With each stride, you shape your narrative, and with each choice, you carve your destiny. Today, let your appearance be a compass guiding you toward the realization of your dreams. You are headed toward a future adorned with accomplishments, happiness, and the fulfillment of your aspirations.

July 18: Today, shine brightly.

July 18 is your day to shine brightly. Embrace your beauty, acknowledge your worth, and let your appearance be a reflection of the incredible person you are. As you navigate this day, remember that you are on a fabulous path, and where you are headed is nothing short of extraordinary. Step into the world with confidence, for you are a beacon of light, illuminating your own way.

July 19: Cultivate courage throughout the day.

As you navigate the hours of today, let courage be a constant companion. In moments of uncertainty, draw strength from the reservoir of courage within. Whether it's a difficult conversation, a new endeavor, or simply facing the unknown, remind yourself that courage is not the absence of doubt but the triumph over it.

Celebrate every small victory, for each one is a testament to your courage. By the end of the day, reflect on the challenges you faced and conquered, recognizing the courageous steps you took. Today is not just a day—it's a journey of courage, and you are the brave explorer charting the course.

July 20: May courage be your companion.

As the day unfolds, may courage be your constant companion. Embrace it as you would a dear friend and watch how it transforms challenges into triumphs. Remember, you are not alone on this journey. Have courage, believe in yourself, and witness the extraordinary unfold. Today, courage is not just a goal—it's a path to discovering the indomitable spirit that resides within you.

July 21: Have faith, you got this!

In the labyrinth of life, faith is the thread that weaves dreams into reality. Believe in yourself, your abilities, and the journey that unfolds before you. Today is not just about facing challenges; it's about embracing them with unwavering faith that you have the strength to navigate whatever comes your way.

Remember, faith is not the absence of challenges but the confidence that you can overcome them. Whatever the day presents, approach it with the assurance that you've got this. Your past triumphs, your resilience, and your inner strength are all testaments to the fact that you are more capable than you realize.

July 22: Be faithful and good faith will come to you.

Faith is a reciprocal force. As you sow the seeds of faith, you reap the fruits of goodness. Be faithful not only to yourself but to the world around you. Cultivate kindness, understanding, and compassion. As you navigate your day, let your actions be infused with the faith that your positive contributions matter.

Good faith is not just a transactional concept; it's a way of living. Trust in the inherent goodness of life, and let that trust guide your interactions with others. By embodying faithfulness, you create a ripple effect of positivity, and in return, good faith finds its way back to you.

July 23: Faith as your guiding light

Throughout the day, let faith serve as your guiding light. In moments of doubt or challenge, remind yourself that faith is the compass that leads you through the storm. Whether faced with decisions, uncertainties, or opportunities, approach each with a heart brimming with faith.

Celebrate the moments of faith—those instances where you trusted in the unseen, believed in your potential or extended kindness to others. Reflect on these moments, for they are the building blocks of a life rich in meaning and purpose.

July 24: May faith illuminate your path.

As you journey through this day, may faith be the gentle breeze beneath your wings. Embrace it, hold onto it, and let it carry you through challenges and triumphs alike. Today, faith is not just a word; it's a practice, a way of being. Have faith, believe in the beauty of your journey, and watch how the universe responds with the embrace of good faith. You've got this, and faith will be your steadfast companion on this extraordinary journey.

July 25: You were courageous the other day.

Take a moment to acknowledge the courage that surged within you recently. Whether it is facing a challenge, making a decision, or embracing vulnerability, recognize that you possess an inner reservoir of bravery. The seeds of courage you planted have already started to blossom, and today is about nurturing that growth.

July 26: Make courage your friend.

Courage is not a distant ally; it is a friend waiting to walk beside you. Embrace it with open arms and invite it into your thoughts and actions. Today is about cultivating a friendship with courage—a friendship that will provide strength in times of doubt, guidance in moments of uncertainty, and resilience in the face of challenges.

Courage is not the absence of fear but the triumph over it. As you face the day's tasks, decisions, and opportunities, let courage be the steady beat of your heart, reminding you of your capability to navigate whatever comes your way.

July 27: Keep going.

In the ebb and flow of life, the journey continues. You've demonstrated courage, and now as you stand on the precipice of today, keep going. Every step is a testament to your resilience, every decision a manifestation of your strength.

Let the momentum of your courage propel you forward. There will be more challenges, more opportunities to be brave, and more moments where you'll need to trust in your capabilities. With courage as your ally, each step becomes a victory, and each new experience is an opportunity for growth.

July 28: Courage: your steadfast companion

Throughout the day, let courage be the whisper in your ear, encouraging you to take bold steps and embrace the unknown. Whether it's a daunting task, a difficult conversation, or an exciting opportunity, face it with the assurance that you have the courage to navigate it successfully.

Reflect on the courageous choices you make today, just as you did the other day. Each one contributes to the narrative of your journey. By evening, acknowledge the courage that propelled you forward and recognize that you are not just moving; you are evolving.

July 29: May courage walk with you today and always.

As you continue your journey on July 29, may courage be the friend that walks beside you. Embrace it, cherish it, and let it infuse your day with the strength to keep going. Your path is illuminated by the light of your courage, and as you venture forth, know that you have a steadfast companion in bravery. Keep going, for every step forward is a testament to the courage that resides within you.

July 30: Happiness comes easy if you smile today.

In the hustle of life, it's easy to forget the power of a smile. Today, make a conscious effort to let happiness in. No matter the challenges or uncertainties, remember that a smile is a small yet potent act that can brighten your day and those around you.

Turn that frown upside down. Life's journey is filled with ups and downs, but the beauty lies in our ability to navigate both with grace. If today feels heavy, turn that frown upside down. Shift your perspective, embrace the positive, and allow your smile to be a beacon of light, dispelling any shadows.

July 31: The ripple effect of a smile

A smile is not just a facial expression; it's a ripple of positivity that extends far beyond. As you smile today, notice how it influences the atmosphere around you. It's contagious, uplifting spirits and creating a chain reaction of joy. Your simple act can make someone else's day a little brighter.

AUGUST

Enjoying the Heat and Finding Strength in the Sweltering Days

August 1: Finding happiness in small moments

Happiness is not always found in grand gestures; sometimes, it resides in the simplicity of a genuine smile. Take a moment to appreciate the small joys around you—the warmth of the sun, the laughter of a friend, or the beauty of the present moment. Let these moments fuel your smile.

August 2: Carry your smile through challenges.

Life may present challenges, but your smile is a constant companion. Carry it with you through the storms, a symbol of your resilience and an affirmation that, despite the difficulties, you choose to find joy. Today, your smile becomes a shield against negativity.

August 3: Share your smile with the world.

As you embrace the day with a smile, consider it a gift not only to yourself but to the world. Share your positivity, radiate kindness, and watch how your smile becomes a source of inspiration for others. In a world that can sometimes be challenging, your smile can be a beacon of hope.

August 4: May your day be illuminated by smiles.

On August 4, let the magic of a smile illuminate your path. Embrace happiness with open arms, turn any frown into a grin, and carry the contagious joy with you. Today is a canvas, and your smile paints it with the vibrant colors of positivity. Embrace the day with a smile, for happiness is just a grin away.

August 5: Touch someone's soul today.

In the vast tapestry of human connection, a simple act of kindness has the power to resonate deeply. Today, make a deliberate effort to touch someone's soul. Extend a genuine compliment, offer a helping hand, or express your appreciation. In the midst of our busy lives, these small gestures can create ripples of joy.

August 6: Make someone feel good today.

As you navigate the day, become a source of positivity for someone else. Whether it's a friend, family member, colleague, or even a stranger, find an opportunity to make them feel good. Your words, actions, and presence can be the catalyst for a brighter moment in their journey.

August 7: In turn, you will feel good inside.

The beauty of kindness lies in its reciprocal nature. As you uplift others, you, too, experience a profound sense of fulfillment. Notice the joy that wells up within you when you witness the positive impact your actions have on someone's day. Today is a reminder that by giving, you receive in abundance.

August 8: The ripple effect of goodness

Every act of kindness creates a ripple effect, spreading positivity far beyond the initial gesture. Today, be a part of this beautiful chain reaction. Your effort to touch someone's soul has the potential to set off a cascade of goodwill, creating a brighter and more compassionate world for us all.

August 9: Simple acts, profound impact

Kindness need not be grand; it thrives in the simplicity of everyday gestures. A smile, a thoughtful word, or a small favor can carry immense weight. In these moments, you have the power to create a positive shift in someone's day, and in doing so, you contribute to a more harmonious world.

August 10: Reflect on the beauty of connection.

As the day unfolds, take a moment to reflect on the beauty of human connection. Consider the smiles you've shared, the uplifted spirits you've encountered, and the warmth you've generated. These are not just fleeting moments but threads that weave a tapestry of compassion and interconnectedness.

August 11: May your day be enriched with soulful connections.

On August 11, embrace the opportunity to touch someone's soul with your kindness. In making others feel good, you contribute to a collective well-being that extends beyond individual moments. Your acts of kindness are not just drops in the ocean; they are waves of positivity that create a lasting impact. Today, let your heart be a beacon of warmth, illuminating the path for both yourself and those you touch with your soulful kindness.

August 12: Let your light shine bright.

In the vast universe of possibilities, you are a luminous presence capable of radiating positivity, warmth, and authenticity. Embrace the metaphorical diamond within you, with facets that represent your individual strengths, talents, and the beauty of your essence. Today, give yourself permission to let that light shine bright.

August 13: Like the brightest star in the night sky.

Imagine yourself as the brightest star, casting its glow across the darkness of the night. Your light has the power to guide, inspire, and bring hope. As you navigate through your day, let your actions, words, and intentions be the celestial light that brightens the lives of those around you.

August 14: Unleash the light inside you.

The light within you is a unique and powerful force waiting to be unleashed. Today, free yourself from any inhibitions or doubts that dim your radiance. Allow the authenticity of your being to emerge, brightening every interaction and leaving traces of inspiration in your wake.

August 15: Radiate positivity and warmth.

Your light is not just a beacon; it's a source of positivity and warmth. Radiate kindness, compassion, and joy. In doing so, you create a welcoming glow that not only transforms your own day but also has a ripple effect, touching the lives of those who cross your path.

August 16: Affirmation: I shine brightly and authentically.

As you stand in the brilliance of your own light, affirm to yourself, "I shine brightly and authentically. My uniqueness is my strength, and I illuminate the world with positivity. I am a beacon of light, guiding others and bringing warmth wherever I go."

August 17: Embrace your brilliance.

Throughout the day, consciously embrace your brilliance. Whether you're faced with challenges or moments of joy, let your light shine through. Celebrate your achievements, acknowledge your resilience, and share your radiance with the world.

August 18: May your light illuminate your path.

On August 18, let your light be a guiding force. Illuminate the path before you with the brightness of your essence. As you shine like a diamond or the brightest star in the night sky, remember that your light is not just an illumination; it's a gift to yourself and others. Embrace the brilliance within you and watch how it transforms your world into a tapestry of vibrant hues and shimmering possibilities.

August 19: The power of inner peace

Inner peace is not a passive state but a powerful force that emanates from within. As you navigate the currents of life, take a moment to center yourself. In the stillness, discover the profound impact that cultivating inner peace can have on your thoughts, emotions, and actions.

August 20: A catalyst for harmony

When you are at peace, your entire world functions in better alignment. Your decisions are grounded, your interactions become more meaningful, and challenges are met with a calm resilience. Inner peace acts as a catalyst, harmonizing the various aspects of your life and creating a balanced, tranquil existence.

August 21: Nurturing your inner sanctuary

Today, make a conscious effort to nurture your inner sanctuary. Engage in practices that bring about a sense of calm—whether it's through meditation, mindful breathing, or moments of quiet reflection. By tending to your inner landscape, you foster an environment where peace can flourish.

August 22: Amidst chaos, find stillness.

Life is a tapestry woven with both calm and chaos. Amidst the turbulence, learn to find stillness within. When you carry inner peace as a steadfast companion, external challenges lose their power to disrupt your equilibrium. You become a beacon of serenity amidst life's storms.

August 23: Affirmation: my inner peace radiates outward.

As you delve into the depths of your inner peace, affirm to yourself, "My inner peace radiates outward, influencing my thoughts, actions, and the world around me. In tranquility, I find strength, and in serenity, I discover clarity."

August 24: The ripple effect of inner peace

The beauty of inner peace is its ability to create a ripple effect. As you cultivate a peaceful existence, you contribute to a more harmonious world. Your interactions, relationships, and endeavors are touched by the gentle influence of tranquility, fostering connections that resonate with understanding and compassion.

August 25: May your world blossom in harmony.

On August 25, nurture the seed of inner peace within your heart. Let it blossom into a vibrant force that transforms your world. As you embrace tranquility, observe how your thoughts align, your emotions settle, and your actions emanate from a place of centeredness. Today is not just about finding inner peace; it's about recognizing the profound impact it has on your entire existence. May your world flourish in the harmonious embrace of inner peace.

August 26: Where there's a will, there's a way.

The journey to success, fulfillment, and personal growth often begins with a resolute will. As you encounter challenges and pursue your goals, remember that the strength of your determination lays the foundation for the path forward. Where there's a will, creativity, and perseverance pave the way, creating avenues that lead to the realization of your aspirations.

August 27: Go that way.

Today, go boldly in the direction of your dreams. Trust the compass of your willpower. Even if the road ahead seems uncertain, your unwavering determination will guide you through the twists and turns. Each step forward is a testament to your commitment, a bridge between where you are now and where you aspire to be.

August 28: Listen to your gut.

Along the journey, pause and listen to the whispers of your gut—the instinctive, intuitive part of you that often knows the way. Your inner voice carries insights, nudging you in the right direction. Trust it, for it is a compass calibrated by your deepest desires and authentic self.

August 29: Affirmation: my willpower fuels my journey.

Affirm to yourself on August 29, "My willpower fuels my journey. I embrace challenges with determination, knowing that where there's a will, there's a way. I trust the path I'm forging, and I listen to the wisdom within."

August 30: Embrace the challenges.

Challenges are not roadblocks but opportunities to exercise your willpower. Embrace them with resilience, viewing each obstacle as a chance to strengthen your resolve. As you navigate challenges, you refine your willpower, making it a potent force that propels you toward your goals.

August 31: Celebrate each step forward.

Willpower is not solely about reaching the destination; it's about the journey and the progress you make along the way. Celebrate each step forward, acknowledging the determination that brought you there. Your journey is a testament to your strength, and every milestone is a victory fueled by your willpower.

May your willpower illuminate your path and let the flame of your willpower illuminate your path. Embrace challenges, trust your instincts, and go confidently toward your dreams. Where there's a will, there's a way, and today is a testament to your unwavering determination. Listen to the call of your inner strength and watch as your journey unfolds with purpose and resilience.

SEPTEMBER

Welcoming Autumns Arrival and the Transition

September 1: Dreams do come true.

In the vast canvas of possibilities, your dreams are the vibrant hues that add depth and meaning to your journey. September is a gentle reminder that the universe responds to the energy you emit. By fostering a belief that dreams can come true, you set in motion a transformative process that aligns your actions, intentions, and energies with the fulfillment of your aspirations.

September 2: Put it out into the universe.

Your thoughts, desires, and intentions carry a resonance that echoes throughout the universe. Today, take a moment to put your dreams out into the cosmos. Whether through visualization, journaling, or heartfelt affirmations, communicate your aspirations with clarity and positivity. The universe is a vast, receptive canvas ready to respond to the brushstrokes of your dreams.

September 3: Nurture the soil of possibility.

Just as a gardener tends to the soil to nurture the growth of flowers, tend to the soil of possibility within your heart. Water your dreams with belief, cultivate them with determination, and let the sunlight of hope illuminate their potential. The more you invest in the fertile ground of your aspirations, the more likely they are to flourish.

September 4: Affirmation: my dreams blossom in the universe.

Affirm to yourself on this day, "My dreams are a powerful force, and as I put them out into the universe, they blossom and flourish. The energy I invest in my dreams returns to me in unexpected and wondrous ways. I trust in the unfolding of my aspirations."

September 5: Witness the flourishing.

As you traverse through the day, be attentive to the subtle signs and synchronicities that align with your dreams. The universe communicates through serendipitous moments, chance encounters, and unexpected opportunities. Witness the flourishing of your dreams as they unfold in ways both subtle and profound.

September 6: Take inspired action.

Putting your dreams into the universe is not only about belief but also about taking inspired action. September encourages you to align your actions with your aspirations. As you step confidently toward your dreams, the universe responds by opening doors, forging connections, and paving the way for your journey.

September 7: May your dreams blossom in abundance.

On September 7, may the energy of your dreams resonate with the universe. Embrace the belief that dreams do come true, and as you put them out into the cosmos, watch with anticipation as they blossom in abundance. Your journey is a dance with the universe, and today, your steps are guided by the rhythm of possibility and fulfillment.

September 8: Believe today.

Belief is the cornerstone of miracles. This day invites you to cultivate a deep and unwavering belief in yourself. Recognize the vast reservoir of potential within, acknowledging that your dreams are not only achievable but also worthy of realization. Today, choose to believe in the magic that resides within you.

September 9: Miracles unfold from self-belief.

Miracles are not reserved for the extraordinary; they are woven into the fabric of your everyday existence. When you believe in yourself, you align with the forces that can turn the ordinary into the extraordinary. Your thoughts, actions, and intentions become the catalyst for the miraculous to unfold in your life.

September 10: The power of self-belief

Self-belief is not a fleeting emotion but a powerful force that shapes your reality. Sept 10 is an affirmation that the more deeply and authentically you believe in your abilities, the more miracles you attract. Your self-belief acts as a magnet, drawing in opportunities, synchronicities, and serendipities that align with your aspirations.

September 11: A day etched into the collective memory of many

It marks the tragic events of the terrorist attacks on the World Trade Center towers in New York City, the Pentagon in Arlington, Virginia, and the crash of Flight 93 in Pennsylvania in 2001.

On this day, we remember the lives lost, the heroism of first responders, and the resilience of the communities affected. It is a solemn day to reflect on the impact of these events on individuals, families, and nations. Let us honor the memory of those who perished, express compassion to those who grieve, and stand united in the pursuit of a world where such acts of violence are replaced by understanding, empathy, and peace.

September 12: Affirmation: I believe in myself and invite miracles.

Affirm to yourself on this day, "I believe in myself, and in this belief, I invite miracles into my life. The magic within me is a guiding force, turning possibilities into realities. I trust in the unfolding of miracles as I walk the path of self-belief."

September 13: Nurture the seed of possibility.

As you move through the day, be mindful of the seed of possibility that self-belief nurtures. Water it with positive thoughts, feed it with affirmations, and bask in the sunlight of your own belief. Just as a well-tended garden flourishes, the garden of your aspirations blossoms with miracles when rooted in self-belief.

September 14: Celebrate every small victory.

Miracles often manifest in the subtlest of ways. Celebrate every small victory, every step forward, and every moment where your belief in yourself has led to positive outcomes. March 16 is a day to recognize that, through self-belief, you are continually sculpting the miraculous landscape of your life.

September 15: May your day be filled with miracles.

On March 16, let the belief in yourself be the cornerstone of the miracles that unfold. Embrace the magic within, trust in your journey, and watch as the ordinary transforms into the extraordinary. Your self-belief is the key to unlocking the door to a world where miracles abound. Today, may you be a witness to the wonders that belief in oneself can manifest.

September 16: The power of positivity

Positivity is a beacon that lights up your path, casting away shadows and inviting warmth into your day. Sept. 16 is a gentle reminder that no matter the circumstances, you hold the power to choose positivity. In every thought, word, and action, let the energy of positivity guide your journey.

Anything positive is better than anything negative in the intricate dance of life. Choose the rhythm of positivity. Sept. 16 encourages you to recognize that, amidst challenges and uncertainties, there are positive aspects waiting to be acknowledged and embraced. Shift your focus toward the bright spots and let them be the canvas upon which you paint your day.

September 17: The ripple effect of positivity

Positivity is not solitary; it has a ripple effect that extends far beyond the individual. As you choose positivity, you contribute to a collective energy of optimism. Your positive actions, words, and thoughts become a gift to yourself and to those around you, creating a harmonious atmosphere.

Affirmation: today, I choose positivity. Affirm to yourself on Sept. 17, "Today, I choose positivity. In every moment, I seek the positive aspects, embrace gratitude, and let joy be my guiding light. My choices today shape the atmosphere of positivity that surrounds me."

September 18: Find joy in the small moments.

Amidst the busyness of the day, take a moment to find joy in the small moments. Whether it's the warmth of sunlight, a kind gesture from a friend, or the simple pleasures of life, let these moments become the building blocks of your positive experience.

September 19: Cultivate a positive perspective.

Positivity is a perspective, and Sept. 19 invites you to cultivate it consciously. When faced with challenges, approach them with a positive mindset. Seek solutions, focus on lessons learned, and view obstacles as stepping stones to growth. Your perspective shapes your reality.

May your day overflow with positivity. Let your day overflow with positivity. Choose to see the good in yourself, in others, and in the world around you. As you consciously navigate your journey with optimism, may the energy of positivity elevate your experiences, creating a tapestry of joy, gratitude, and fulfillment. Today, remember that the power to choose positivity is within you, and it can transform the ordinary into the extraordinary.

The power of positivity is a beacon that lights up your path, casting away shadows and inviting warmth into your day. September 19 is a gentle reminder that no matter the circumstances, you hold the power to choose positivity. In every thought, word, and action, let the energy of positivity guide your journey.

September 20: Anything positive is better than anything negative.

In the intricate dance of life, choose the rhythm of positivity. September 20 encourages you to recognize that, amidst challenges and uncertainties, there are positive aspects waiting to be acknowledged and embraced. Shift your focus toward the bright spots, and let them be the canvas upon which you paint your day.

The ripple effect of positivity is not solitary; it has a ripple effect that extends far beyond the individual. As you choose positivity, you contribute to a collective energy of optimism. Your positive actions, words, and thoughts become a gift to yourself and to those around you, creating a harmonious atmosphere.

September 21: Affirmation: today, I choose positivity.

Affirm to yourself on September 21, "Today, I choose positivity. In every moment, I seek the positive aspects, embrace gratitude, and let joy be my guiding light. My choices today shape the atmosphere of positivity that surrounds me."

September 22: Find joy in the small moments.

Amidst the busyness of the day, take a moment to find joy in the small moments. Whether it's the warmth of sunlight, a kind gesture from a friend, or the simple pleasures of life, let these moments become the building blocks of your positive experience.

September 23: Cultivate a positive perspective.

Positivity is a perspective, and September 23 invites you to cultivate it consciously. When faced with challenges, approach them with a positive mindset. Seek solutions, focus on lessons learned, and view obstacles as stepping stones to growth. Your perspective shapes your reality.

May your day overflow with positivity. Let your day overflow with positivity. Choose to see the good in yourself, in others, and in the world around you. As you consciously navigate your journey with optimism, may the energy of positivity elevate your experiences, creating a tapestry of joy, gratitude, and fulfillment. Today, remember that the power to choose positivity is within you, and it can transform the ordinary into the extraordinary.

September 24: Let your inner child guide you.

Within each of us resides an inner child—an essence of pure authenticity, curiosity, and joy. Today, allow your inner child to take the reins. Reconnect with the simplicity and wonder that your younger self embodied. Let the enthusiasm and intuition of your inner child guide you toward decisions and activities that resonate with your true self.

Trust my inner voice and embrace my inner child.

Affirm to yourself on September 24, "I trust my inner voice, and today, I embrace the wisdom of my inner child. In tuning in to my intuition, I rediscover the joy, creativity, and authenticity within me. My inner child guides me toward a path filled with genuine happiness and self-discovery."

September 25: Reignite the spark of curiosity.

Your inner child is a beacon of curiosity. September 25 is an opportunity to reignite the spark of curiosity within you. Explore new ideas, try activities that once brought you joy, and approach challenges with the fresh perspective of a child discovering the world for the first time.

September 26: Celebrate playfulness and creativity.

Children approach life with a sense of playfulness and boundless creativity. Today, infuse your day with elements of play and creative expression. Whether it's engaging in a playful activity, pursuing a creative project, or simply allowing your imagination to soar, let your inner child be the source of inspiration.

September 27: Embrace spontaneity and authenticity.

Your inner child thrives on spontaneity and authenticity. September 27 encourages you to embrace these qualities. Be spontaneous in your decisions, allowing room for unexpected joys. Authenticity is your guiding light—express your true self without reservation and watch how it transforms your interactions and experiences.

September 28: May your inner child illuminate the path ahead.

On September 28, let the wisdom of your inner voice and the guidance of your inner child illuminate the path ahead. Listen closely to the whispers of intuition, follow the sparks of joy, and embrace the authenticity that comes from connecting with your inner child. Today is not just a day—it's a celebration of rediscovering the vibrant, playful, and authentic aspects of yourself. May your journey be guided by the wisdom and joy that reside within.

September 29: The seed of positive thoughts

Your mind is a garden, and positive thoughts are the seeds that you plant. September 29 encourages you to be intentional about cultivating a mindset that fosters optimism, gratitude, and hope. Just as a tiny seed holds the potential to grow into a mighty tree, your positive thoughts bear the promise of a flourishing and fulfilling life.

September 30: The equilibrium of positive emotions

Positive thoughts act as the catalyst for positive emotions. As you nurture an optimistic perspective, you create an internal equilibrium of joy, resilience, and gratitude. September 30 is an invitation to consciously choose thoughts that uplift your spirits, allowing vibrant hues of positivity to color your emotional landscape.

My thoughts shape my reality.

Affirm to yourself on September 30, "My thoughts have the power to shape my reality. Today, I choose positivity. I sow the seeds of optimism, and as they grow, they create a vibrant garden of positive emotions and actions in my daily life."

OCTOBER

Embracing the Positivity of the Pumpkin Season

October 1: Get up, get going, move that body any way you can.

On this energizing day, October 1, ignite your spirit. Rise, move, and feel the vitality coursing through you. Whether a gentle stretch or a dynamic workout, honor your body's ability to move. Today, embrace the joy that comes from simply being in motion.

October 2: Do not look back on yesterday. Keep moving forward. One step at a time.

In the journey of October 2, focus on the path ahead. Resist the urge to dwell on yesterday's chapters. With each step forward, you craft the story of today and tomorrow. One step at a time, with determination and resilience, move confidently into the boundless possibilities of the future.

October 3: Breathe in the fresh air and fill your lungs with all the nature around us.

Amidst the beauty of October 3, pause to reconnect with nature. Inhale deeply, absorbing the freshness that surrounds you. Let the air rejuvenate your spirit and remind you of the profound harmony that exists between you and the natural world. Today, find solace in the simple act of breathing in the essence of nature.

October 4: Take the chance you've been putting off. Do it today; do not wait until tomorrow; it may never come.

October 4 invites courage into your life. Seize the opportunity you've hesitated on. Today is the day to take that chance, embark on that adventure, or pursue that dream. Embrace the now, for tomorrow is uncertain. Let today be the canvas upon which you paint your aspirations.

October 5: Challenges will arise; keep moving forward.

In the face of challenges on October 5, be steadfast. Each obstacle is a stepping stone on your journey. Embrace resilience, adaptability, and an unwavering spirit. As challenges arise, remember that you have the strength to keep moving forward, one step at a time.

October 6: Thoughts create how you feel and how your day will go. So make them count.

On October 6, acknowledge the power of your thoughts. They shape your emotions and influence the course of your day. Choose positivity, cultivate gratitude, and let your thoughts be a guiding force for a day filled with joy, purpose, and fulfillment.

October 7: Be insightful today.

In the realm of October 7, cultivate insight. Observe the world around you with curiosity and understanding. Be receptive to the nuances of your experiences. Today, let insight be your companion, guiding you to deeper connections, profound realizations, and a richer appreciation for the beauty of life.

October 8: Do not look back in the rearview mirror; keep watching in front of you.

October 8 is a reminder to focus on the road ahead. Resist the temptation to dwell on the past. Your journey is unfolding in the present and future. Keep your eyes forward, embrace the possibilities that lie ahead, and let the rearview mirror serve only as a reflection, not a distraction.

October 9: Do what you desire. This is your screenplay.

On this liberating day, October 9, recognize that life is your canvas, and you are the author of your own screenplay. Embrace the freedom to pursue what you truly desire. Let passion and purpose guide your choices, and write a story filled with scenes that resonate with joy, fulfillment, and authenticity. Today, the script is in your hands—make it uniquely yours.

October 10: October is going to be a beautiful month if you think positively.

On October 10, set the tone for a beautiful month by embracing positivity. Your thoughts shape your reality, and as you choose optimism, you invite beauty, joy, and fulfillment into your October journey. Cultivate a positive mindset, and let the month unfold with a tapestry of uplifting moments.

October 11: Look how far you have come. Keep putting one foot in front of the other.

In the reflection of October 11, acknowledge your journey. Take pride in the progress you've made and appreciate how far you've come. With each step, you've overcome challenges and embraced growth. Keep putting one foot in front of the other, for the path ahead is illuminated by your resilience and determination.

October 12: Organize something today that you feel has gotten out of control lately.

Today, restore order in a space that may have felt chaotic. Whether physical or mental, organizing brings clarity. Tackle a task that has seemed overwhelming and regain a sense of control. As you bring order, you create a harmonious foundation for the days ahead.

October 13: Set goals and watch them flourish. Achieve something good today.

On this empowering day, become the architect of your aspirations. Set goals that resonate with your dreams and witness them flourish into reality. Today, channel your energy into achieving something good—something that aligns with your values and propels you forward on the path to success. You have the power to turn your aspirations into accomplishments. Seize the day!

October 14: You can only change you. You know what is locked up inside you.

On October 14, embrace the power of self-transformation. Recognize that the key to change lies within you. Unlock the potential that is tucked away inside and take deliberate steps toward becoming the best version of yourself. You have the ability to shape your own narrative.

October 15: Let go of those chains that are holding you back.

In the liberation of October 15, release the chains that hinder your progress. Identify what holds you back—be it fear, doubt, or past burdens—and choose to let go. Free yourself from constraints, and as you do, open the door to new possibilities and a future unburdened by the weight of the past.

October 16: Gratitude is the key in everyday life for you to see the good in all.

On October 16, unlock the door to a positive perspective through gratitude. Embrace the transformative power of appreciating the good in everyday life. By fostering a grateful mindset, you illuminate the beauty that surrounds you and invite joy into each moment.

October 17: Be grateful going into this month. Life is like chapters.

As you enter October 17, carry gratitude as your companion. Life unfolds like chapters in a book, each bringing unique experiences. Embrace the journey with appreciation for the lessons, the joys, and the growth. Cultivate gratitude, for it is the key that unlocks the fullness of each chapter in your life story.

October 18: On this day, think of success and how it often comes with persistence and dedication. Balance your passion for something that excites you.

Celebrate October 18 as a day of reflection on success. Acknowledge the role of persistence and dedication in achieving your goals. Embrace the balance between your passion and the commitment required for success. Today, let the spirit of determination fuel your journey toward the aspirations that ignite your excitement.

October 19: Today, stay focused on your goals and find a balance that works for you.

On October 19, anchor yourself in focus. Amidst the myriad of tasks and aspirations, find the equilibrium that works uniquely for you. Stay committed to your goals, and in the pursuit of balance, discover the harmony that allows you to navigate challenges with resilience and savor the joys of your achievements.

October 20: What you give is what you will get back in this life we call our journey.

On this insightful day, contemplate the essence of reciprocity in life's journey. Recognize that the energy, kindness, and generosity you invest in others often find their way back to you. Today, let your actions be a reflection of the positivity you wish to receive and embrace the interconnected dance of giving and receiving in the beautiful tapestry of life.

October 21: Goals are important.

On this purposeful day, October 21, acknowledge the significance of setting and pursuing goals. Goals give direction to your journey, providing a roadmap for growth and achievement. Today, reflect on your aspirations and take deliberate steps toward the goals that shape your path.

October 22: Follow your path and live in the moment.

In the embrace of October 22, honor your journey. Follow your own unique path, guided by authenticity and purpose. Today, immerse yourself in the present moment, allowing the beauty of now to unfold. Your journey is a collection of these moments—cherish them, savor them, and live fully in the grace of the present.

October 23: Have a purpose, a "why" in this journey we call "life." Help others, and you will reap what you sow.

On October 23, cultivate a purpose in your journey. Define your "why" and let it guide your actions. Extend a helping hand to others, for in doing so, you sow seeds that will grow into a harvest of fulfillment and meaningful connections.

October 24: Inspire others; do not be jealous of what they have and you want.

In the spirit of October 24, be a source of inspiration. Celebrate the successes of others without envy. Your genuine support and encouragement not only uplift them but also contribute to a positive and harmonious atmosphere.

October 25: When you do good, you feel good on the inside, and outward will show that.

On October 25, embrace the beauty of doing good. Acts of kindness not only make a positive impact on others but also create a sense of fulfillment within yourself. Today, let your actions reflect the goodness that resides in your heart.

October 26: When you are aligned with your inner self and inner purpose, you will be much more in tune and positive, like an instrument that has been fine-tuned.

October 26 calls for alignment. Tune in to your inner self, identify your purpose, and let the symphony of positivity resonate within you. When you are in harmony with your authentic self, life becomes a melody of fulfillment.

October 27: The wise are always looking and listening.

On this day of wisdom, cultivate the art of observation. Stay attuned to the world around you, listen deeply, and absorb the lessons life has to offer. The wise are perpetual learners, always seeking understanding and insight.

October 28: Accept yourself how you are.

In the spirit of October 28, practice self-acceptance. Embrace your unique qualities, recognizing that your authenticity is your strength. When you accept yourself as you are, you pave the way for growth, confidence, and a genuine connection with others.

October 29: Free yourself and break down those walls holding you back today.

On this liberating day, October 29, recognize the barriers that may be constraining your progress. Take courageous steps to dismantle those walls. Embrace the freedom that comes with breaking free from limitations and allow the expansiveness of possibility to shape your journey. Today, set yourself free from the confines that hinder your potential.

October 30: As this month comes to a close, look forward, not backward.

On this reflective day, October 30, turn your gaze toward the future. Resist the urge to dwell on the past month's chapters. Instead, focus on the opportunities that lie ahead. With optimism as your compass, step into the new month with anticipation and a heart open to the possibilities that await. Embrace the journey that unfolds in the pages yet to be written.

October 31: Harvest or Halloween is today. Embrace the season's spirit.

On this festive day, October 31, celebrate the bounties of the harvest or immerse yourself in the playful spirit of Halloween. Embrace the richness of the season, whether through the gathering of abundance or the joyous festivities. Let the day be filled with warmth, gratitude, and the delight of shared moments. Today, savor the unique flavors that October 31 brings and welcome the changing seasons with open arms.

NOVEMBER

Have Gratitude and Be Thankful for Harvest Time

November 1: All you need to start this month is already within you. You are blossoming over these months that have passed, and that is preparing you for.

At this beginning of November, recognize the inner strength and growth that resides within you. Every step you've taken in the past months has been a preparation for the opportunities and challenges this new month brings. Embrace the abundance within, and step into November with confidence and resilience. Your journey is continually blossoming, and you are well-prepared for the chapters ahead.

November 2: Embrace the power of positivity.

Today, let positivity be your guiding light. Focus on the good that surrounds you and allow optimism to shape your outlook. In choosing to see the bright side, you not only uplift yourself but also inspire those around you.

November 3: Cultivate gratitude in every moment.

Gratitude is the key to abundance. Take a moment today to appreciate the simple joys and the people who bring warmth to your life. As you cultivate gratitude, you sow the seeds for a harvest of positivity.

November 4: Find strength in every challenge.

Challenges are opportunities in disguise. Approach difficulties with resilience, knowing that each hurdle is a chance for growth. You have the strength within you to overcome anything that comes your way.

November 5: Radiate kindness.

In a world where you can be anything, be kind. Extend a helping hand, share a smile, and spread positivity wherever you go. Your acts of kindness have a ripple effect, creating a brighter world for everyone.

November 6: Cherish your progress.

Reflect on the progress you've made so far. Celebrate both the small and significant victories. Acknowledge the journey you've undertaken, for each step is a testament to your resilience and determination.

November 7: Nurture self-compassion.

Be kind to yourself today. Understand that you are a work in progress, and growth comes at its own pace. Nurture self-compassion, and let self-love be the foundation upon which you build a positive and fulfilling life.

November 8: Share your light with others.

Your light can brighten the darkest corners. Today, share your positivity with others. Whether through a kind word, a gesture, or a smile, let your light shine and inspire those who may need it most.

November 9: Embrace change as a catalyst for growth.

Change is the only constant in life. Embrace it as a catalyst for growth and transformation. Today, see opportunities in every change, knowing that each shift propels you toward becoming the best version of yourself.

November 10: Visualize your best self.

Close your eyes and visualize the person you aspire to be. Envision your goals, dreams, and the positive impact you can make. As you visualize your best self, you set the stage for the incredible journey ahead.

November 11: Give grace in all you do and be a guiding light to others.

Today, practice grace in your actions and interactions. Approach challenges with poise and extend understanding to those around you. Be a guiding light, illuminating the path for others with your kindness and compassion.

November 12: What you give today will come back to you in tenfold.

Embrace the law of reciprocity today. The positive energy and kindness you sow into the world will return to you manifold. Be generous with your spirit and watch as the universe responds with abundance and blessings.

November 13: Organization is the key to unlocking your full potential.

Start by decluttering your physical space. A tidy environment paves the way for a focused mind. Arrange your surroundings like the stage for a star, creating a backdrop that enhances your shine.

November 14: Now let's fuel that sparkle with motivation.

Set achievable goals for the day, each one a stepping stone toward your larger aspirations. Break down your tasks into manageable steps, and let the satisfaction of completing them propel you forward. Remember, a star doesn't shy away from the spotlight; it thrives in it.

November 15: Thoughts create your reality.

Today, remember the incredible power of your thoughts. Your mind is a creator, shaping the reality you experience. Focus on the things in life that you want, that align with your purpose, and that bring you joy. Redirect your energy away from the things that don't serve your purpose and watch as your positive thoughts shape a reality filled with abundance and fulfillment. You have the ability to manifest the life you desire through the thoughts you choose to cultivate.

November 16: Trust the process.

In the vast tapestry of life, your focus today is on trusting the process. Believe that things will align in your favor. Embrace the journey with confidence, knowing that every twist and turn is guiding you toward your destination. Trust in your resilience, trust in the lessons, and trust that the universe is working in your favor. As you trust the process, you open yourself up to the endless possibilities that lie ahead.

November 17: Be calm and still today.

In the tranquility of today, be calm and still. Amidst the hustle and bustle, find a moment of serenity. Know that everything you want is on its way to you, even if it doesn't feel like it at this moment. Trust in the timing of your life and believe that the universe is orchestrating beautiful outcomes on your behalf. Allow patience and peace to accompany you as you await the arrival of your desires. The journey is unfolding, and your dreams are on the way.

November 18: You are what you want to come into your life.

Disregard the doubters and naysayers, for whoever told you that you can't do it is wrong. Take that disbelief and transform it into a declaration. Affirm to yourself, "I am what I want to come into my life." You have the power to shape your reality and be exactly what your inner voice tells you. Embrace your dreams, believe in your capabilities, and confidently step into the role of the person you aspire to become. Today, let self-belief drown out the noise of negativity and affirm your ability to manifest your desires. You are the architect of your destiny.

November 19: Gratitude paves the way for Thanksgiving.

In this month of Thanksgiving, let's embrace gratitude in our hearts. Take a moment to reflect on the abundance in your life, the love that surrounds you, and the opportunities that await. As we prepare to sit at the table with our family, let's rejoice in gratitude, casting away resentment. Today, express thanks for the blessings, both big and small, and foster a spirit of appreciation that sets the stage for a joyous and harmonious Thanksgiving celebration with loved ones.

November 20: Confidence is silent, insecurity is loud.

In the symphony of life, let your confidence be the quiet strength that guides you. Today, on November 20, allow your actions to speak louder than words. Confidence is silent, a powerful force that emanates from within. Stand tall, speak your truth with assurance, and let your deeds resonate. Insecurity may clamor for attention, but you, in your quiet confidence, exude a magnetic strength that effortlessly draws positivity and respect. Today, show the world the grace and power that reside within a silent, confident heart.

November 21: Decode the silent cry for value and respect.

Recognize that defensiveness often conceals a silent plea for acknowledgment and respect. On this day, November 21, strive to decode the unspoken needs of those around you. Be a source of understanding and compassion, offering value and respect to those who may be silently seeking it. In embracing empathy, you cultivate connections and contribute to a world where everyone feels seen and appreciated. Today, let your actions speak volumes, echoing the importance of valuing and respecting one another.

November 22: Embrace mistakes as learning curves.

On this day, November 22, acknowledge and embrace your mistakes. Instead of denying them, see them as valuable learning curves on the journey of life. Mistakes are not roadblocks; they are stepping stones that pave your way to growth and wisdom. Learn from them, let them shape you, and move forward with the newfound knowledge that propels you toward becoming the best version of yourself. Today, celebrate the lessons hidden within the errors and allow them to guide you toward continuous improvement.

November 23: Cultivate compassion by letting go of defensiveness.

Discover the profound truth that compassion and defensiveness cannot coexist. On this day, November 23, embark on a journey of learning. Understand that true compassion blossoms when you let go of defensiveness. By opening your heart to understanding, you create space for empathy and connection. Today, release the need to shield yourself, and in doing so, discover the transformative power of compassion that bridges hearts and fosters unity.

November 24: If you want change, start with yourself.

In the pursuit of change, remember the profound wisdom: if you want change, start with yourself. On this day, November 24, reflect on the areas where you can grow and evolve. Be the catalyst for the transformation you seek in your life and in the world around you. By embracing change within, you set the stage for positive shifts that resonate far beyond.

November 25: Let's all give thanks for all we have.

On this day of gratitude, November 25, let's join in a collective chorus of thanks. Take a moment to appreciate the abundance that surrounds you, the love that uplifts you, and the blessings that grace your life. Gratitude is a powerful force that magnifies joy. As we give thanks for all we have, let the spirit of appreciation weave through our hearts, creating a tapestry of warmth and connection.

November 26: Choose strength over rudeness.

Reflect on this truth: rudeness is the weak person's imitation of strength. On this November 26, gaze inward. Evaluate how you choose to express yourself. Opt for the genuine strength that lies in kindness, understanding, and empathy. Today, let your actions be a reflection of your true strength—one that uplifts and inspires, fostering a positive atmosphere around you.

November 27: Embrace authenticity and truth.

As you journey through today, November 27, take a moment to look inside yourself. Share your authentic self with others, for in truth lies a genuine connection. Understand that the truth can be challenging, for it has the power to unravel illusions. Despite this, strive to foster a space where authenticity thrives. People may resist hearing the truth at times, but in doing so, they safeguard their illusions. As you navigate conversations, let your commitment to truth be a beacon of honesty and sincerity. In embracing authenticity, you cultivate relationships built on genuine understanding.

November 28: Unlock the chains that bind us.

Recognize that each of us carries a battle, a twist in our minds, a challenge that may torment us. On this November 28, acknowledge imperfection as a universal truth. Together, let's strive to "unlock the chains that bind us." Refuse to be a victim of circumstance, and instead, empower yourself to break free from the constraints that hold you back. In fostering understanding and compassion, we build a supportive community that uplifts and encourages each other's journey toward healing and growth.

November 29: Escape the bottomless pit of resentment.

Consider resentment as a bottomless pit where no one deserves to live. On November 29, seize the opportunity to explore the escape routes that life offers. There are plenty of paths to freedom, each leading to a brighter and more fulfilling destination. Embrace forgiveness, understanding, and compassion as tools to pave your way out of resentment. Today, choose the liberating journey that opens doors to joy, peace, and a heart unburdened by the weight of grudges.

November 30: Reflecting on the month

In concluding this month, take a brief moment today, November 30, to look back. Reflect on the lessons learned, the growth experienced, and the moments that brought joy. Acknowledge the challenges overcome and celebrate the victories, both big and small. As you pause to contemplate, carry the wisdom of this month into the journey that lies ahead. May the reflections of November pave the way for a December filled with positivity, growth, and renewed determination.

DECEMBER

Let's Spread Positivity and Light

December 1: Embrace the gift of a new month.

On this first day of December, let us refrain from dwelling on the past. Instead, turn your gaze toward the opportunities that this new month brings. Embrace the joy and presents it holds, ready to unwrap each day with a sense of wonder and enthusiasm. December is a chapter waiting to be written; let it be filled with positivity, growth, and the warmth of festive moments. Today marks the beginning of a journey into a month of endless possibilities.

December 2: Rise above comparison.

On this day, December 2, resist the urge to feel left behind or succumb to jealousy. Comparison is a thief of joy, and the seeds of envy can sprout quickly like thorns that harm. Instead, celebrate the unique journey you're on. Embrace the achievements and joys of others without allowing them to overshadow your own path. Rise above comparison, for your journey is one of individual growth and fulfillment. Let the warmth of contentment replace the cold grip of envy, nurturing a body and mind free from the burden of ill feelings.

December 3: Shine bright in every color of the rainbow.

On this radiant day, December 3, allow yourself to shine in every color of the rainbow. Embrace the diversity of your emotions, experiences, and aspirations. Let your unique brilliance light up this month, just like the festive lights that illuminate the holiday season. Celebrate the tapestry of life, filled with joy, love, and opportunities. Today, be a beacon of positivity, and may your vibrant spirit create a joyful atmosphere as we approach the celebrations that December holds for each of us.

December 4: Honoring ourselves as the year closes.

As the year gracefully approaches its close, let's take a moment on this fourth day of December to honor ourselves. Praise the resilience that guided us through challenges, celebrate the growth that emerged from lessons, and acknowledge the strength that carried us through the highs and lows. Today, let self-appreciation fill your heart as you recognize the unique journey you've traveled. December is a time for reflection and gratitude, a chance to honor the beautiful tapestry of experiences that have shaped you throughout the year.

December 5: Embrace honor and unity.

On this fifth day of December, let the spirit of honor envelop us. Recognize that every triumph, every challenge met, and every step taken deserves acknowledgment. Let's extend the embrace of family to all, fostering unity and connection. Today, know that the light within you is meant to shine. Embrace your unique brilliance, and may our collective radiance illuminate the path of togetherness and shared joy. In honoring ourselves and each other, we weave a tapestry of strength and unity.

December 6: Gratitude for the journey and radiant light

On this wonderful day, December 6, let's make it great. Take a moment to thank ourselves for all we've surpassed this year. Each challenge met and every obstacle overcome has contributed to our growth. As we bask in gratitude for the journey, let's continue to give our ray of light to all we meet. Be a source of positivity, kindness, and inspiration, spreading warmth and joy to illuminate the paths of others. December 6 is an opportunity to shine brightly and share the radiance of our journey with the world.

December 7: Find the light to guide us.

A beautiful sentiment. On this day, finding the light within can indeed guide us through challenging times. Finding the light within ourselves can be a powerful source of strength and guidance, especially during challenging times. It's a beautiful sentiment that emphasizes the importance of inner resilience, positivity, and hope. When we tap into our own inner light, we often discover the strength and courage needed to navigate through difficulties and emerge stronger on the other side. It's a reminder that even in the darkest moments, there's a potential for personal growth and transformation.

December 8: Nostalgia

As the winter winds weave through the air, there's a magical allure that December holds. It's not just the frost-kissed windows or the soft blankets of snow, but it's a warmth that transcends time—nostalgia.

Today, let's embrace the enchantment of nostalgia, like being surrounded by the familiar embrace of home during the holidays. Picture the crackling fireplace, the scent of cinnamon, and the laughter that echoes through the halls. In these moments, time feels like a companion, gently guiding us back to the cherished memories of our past.

December 9: As you open the door

As you open the door to your home or step into the world beyond, let the spirit of December 9 be one of positivity and love. Every person who walks through your door carries a story, a journey that deserves acknowledgment and warmth. Approach each encounter with the open arms of family, even if they're not bound by blood. Remember, we are all interconnected, sharing this beautiful journey of life.

So let love be the ornament that adorns your conversations, understanding the tinsel that wraps around your encounters. Spread kindness like snowflakes, unique and gentle, leaving a touch of magic wherever you go.

December 10: As you venture forth into this day, carry the nostalgia with you, whether or not you are home or just in your heart but in your actions.

Be the reason someone feels the warmth of a December night, the reason someone smiles at the echoes of laughter, and the reason someone believes in the magic of this season.

May the doors you enter through and those who enter yours be greeted with the love and joy inspired by December 10. Today, let's build bridges of connection, knit together by threads of shared memories and the promise of many more to come.

December 11: As we traverse the tapestry of time

There exists a beautiful belief that transcends the boundaries between the mortal and the divine. In the realm of hope and spirituality, the notion takes root that when our earthly journey concludes, we embark on a celestial transformation. On this day, a symphony of celestial energies converges, casting a gentle glow of reassurance upon our lives. It is a belief that when we depart this world, we metamorphose into benevolent angels tasked with watching over our loved ones. On December 11, let us embrace the comforting thought that the spirits of those we hold dear are by our side, manifesting as guardian angels, casting their protective gaze upon us from the ethereal realms. May this day be a celebration of enduring connections and the everlasting presence of love that transcends the boundaries of time and space.

December 12: Life unfolds with purpose.

Within its intricate design, we find ourselves embarking on unique journeys. As humans, we're bound to make mistakes, face failures, and navigate the twists of our individual paths. Yet in these moments of adversity, we discover the profound strength within us. We embrace the wisdom that comes from learning, rise resiliently from setbacks, and triumph over challenges. Today, let us acknowledge our shared human experience, recognizing that each stumble is a step toward growth, and every hurdle surmounted is a testament to our indomitable spirit.

December 13: Embrace the beauty of life's journey

Let's start this day with an affirmation, "Today, I acknowledge the ebb and flow of people in my life. Just as the tide brings in new faces, it also carries others away. Each person leaves an imprint, a lesson, or a blessing. I am here for a purpose, and every encounter, whether joyous or challenging, is a part of my unique journey.

In moments of triumph, I celebrate the beauty of life, grateful for the abundance that surrounds me. During challenging times, I find strength in knowing that lessons are hidden within adversity. Every experience is a thread woven into the intricate tapestry of my existence.

Today, I release the need for right or wrong answers in my journey. Instead, I embrace the uncertainty, understanding that growth often sprouts from the unexpected. I am thankful for the diverse experiences that shape my character and deepen my understanding of the world.

Whether the sun shines brightly or clouds cast shadows, I am grateful for the gift of today. Each moment is a chance to learn, to love, and to live fully. I welcome the beauty of life's unpredictable path, knowing that every step contributes to the masterpiece of my unique story.

I am open to the lessons, joys, and connections that this day brings. With gratitude in my heart, I embrace the ever-unfolding journey of life."

December 14: Embrace my unique journey.

Today, I reflect on the roads I have traveled, the paths I have chosen, and the journey that has brought me to this moment. Every decision, every turn, has contributed to the person I am today.

I acknowledge that I may carry regrets from certain choices, roads that seemed promising but led to disappointment. Today, I choose to release the weight of those regrets. I recognize that every road, whether paved with success or marked by challenges, has shaped my character and brought valuable lessons.

If there were exits I took that led to dark roads, I forgive myself. I understand that those detours were part of my growth, and today, I let go of any lingering shadows. I choose to focus on the light at the end of the road, the hope that guides me forward.

December 15: A reminder that I am exactly where I am meant to be

Every twist and turn has led me to this point, and I honor the resilience and strength that brought me here. Today, I celebrate my unique journey, appreciating the mosaic of experiences that make me whole.

I am grateful for the roads that made me happy and the ones that challenged me. Each road has contributed to the depth and richness of my life. As I continue on my path, I embrace the present moment, knowing that the journey is ongoing and I always have the power to find the light at the end of the road.

December 16: Today's reminder

You cannot control others. Anything you do or say gets filtered through the lens of whatever they are going through at that moment. Remember, it is not your problem. Just keep doing your thing with as much integrity, passion, and love as possible.

As you embark on today's journey, I am reminded of the inherent truth that I cannot control the actions, reactions, or perspectives of others. Every individual carries their own set of experiences, emotions, and circumstances, shaping the way they perceive and respond to the world.

December 17: In moments of interaction, it's crucial to acknowledge that your words and actions may be interpreted through the unique filter of another person's reality.

Say this as an affirmation, "Today, I release the burden of trying to control outcomes beyond my influence."

December 18: Instead, you should choose to focus on your own path.

On this day, be guided by principles of integrity, passion, and love. By staying true to oneself and nurturing the positive energy within, you can navigate through challenges with grace and authenticity.

Today's mantra: "I release the need to control others. I embrace my journey with integrity, passion, and love."

December 19: May this reminder serve as a guiding light.

Today, allow to approach the day with a sense of inner peace and purpose.
Affirmation: "Today, I am allowing myself to approach the day with a profound sense of inner peace and purpose. I embrace the positivity that flows within, guiding me toward fulfilling my goals with clarity and joy."

December 20: Daily affirmation

Not everyone will be happy for you, and that's okay. Understand that their happiness, or lack thereof, is a reflection of their inner world, not yours. Like the rising sun that brings light to the world, focus on your own growth and positivity. Just as the sun rises each morning, not everyone is awake to witness it. In the same way, not everyone will appreciate or support your journey. Let peace be with you today, knowing that your path is unique and your happiness is not dependent on the approval of others. Embrace the warmth of your own light and continue to rise, regardless of who may still be asleep in the darkness. Shine bright and let the peace within you guide your day.

December 21: Find inspiration in the beauty of nature and the symbolism of growth.

Today, envision a future where, like a tree, You can provide shade, shelter, and nourishment to those around you.

In your mind's eye, see yourself as a majestic tree, branches stretching out with abundant fruit. This image feels like a divine sign, a message from something greater than yourself. Perhaps it's a call to cultivate love and kindness within, much like a tree bearing fruits for others.

December 22: Believe that when your time in this world comes to an end, you will transform into a loving and beautiful tree.

Those who come across your tree will be blessed with the fruits of positivity, joy, and good luck.

Life is unpredictable, and we never know who will find solace beneath our branches. Embrace the uncertainty, knowing that whoever seeks refuge under your tree will find a moment of peace and be nourished by the positivity you have cultivated throughout your journey.
May the seeds of kindness I plant today grow into a flourishing tree of love, providing sustenance to those in need. As I imagine this beautiful tree, I am reminded of the interconnectedness of all living things and the ripple effect of our actions.

December 23: Today, I commit to nurturing the seeds of goodness within fostering a legacy that extends beyond your time here.

Aspire to be a source of blessings for others, just as my imagined tree stands as a symbol of hope and abundance.

May the fruit of your tree bring joy and prosperity to those who encounter it, creating a ripple of positivity that extends far beyond my wildest dreams.

December 24: Today, embrace the transformative power of perspective.

Instead of dwelling on life's undeserved misfortunes, choose to see them as opportunities for growth and new beginnings.

In the face of challenges, recognize the potential for these difficulties to open doors to beautiful, unexplored chapters in your life story. Each misfortune, though initially undeserved, becomes a stepping stone to a richer and more fulfilling narrative.

Be resilient and hold the power to turn adversity into strength. As you face the unexpected twists and turns of life, be reminded that every closed door is an invitation to find a new entrance, a fresh start.

December 25: With each challenge

You are sculpting the narrative of your life, molding it into a story of resilience, courage, and triumph. The misfortunes that come my way are not roadblocks but rather opportunities for you to showcase my inner strength and resilience.

You are the author of your life and choose to craft a tale of perseverance and growth. As you face each new challenge, unlock the potential within yourself to create something beautiful from the unexpected.

December 26: Affirm that life's misfortunes are not the end but the beginning of a new and exciting chapter.

Open to the possibilities that lie beyond every closed door, and trust that the universe is guiding you toward a story filled with resilience, joy, and unexpected blessings.

You are worthy and always supported. If you can dream it, you can do it. Envision what you want, and it will be meant for you.

December 27: In life, it's crucial to prioritize your own journey and aspirations.

Ultimately, everyone tends to prioritize their own well-being, and if you're constantly preoccupied with the concerns of others, you may find yourself feeling isolated when you need support. This realization led me to commit to consistency, to listen to my own needs, and to make choices that align with my best interests. It's not about being uncaring or selfish but rather acknowledging the importance of self-care and personal growth. Taking this stance empowers me to navigate life with a clear focus on my own path while still being mindful of the needs of others.

December 28: Wrapping up December

Don't let anyone dull your sparkle! Embrace the brilliance within you and let your unique light shine brightly. Your authenticity is your strength, and as you navigate life's journey, remember that you have the power to illuminate even the darkest corners. Shine with confidence, and let your radiant energy inspire those around you. Your sparkle is a reflection of your resilience, joy, and unwavering spirit. So stand tall, embrace your individuality, and let the world witness the extraordinary glow that is uniquely yours.

December 29: In the end, your thoughts shape your actions.

Here exists a connection between understanding and application, between belief and responsibility. Your contemplation guides your behavior, and the knowledge you acquire influences the way you live. "My prayer is that whoever is your God, that he molds us into believers who prioritize thoughtful consideration, leading to purposeful action." May we first be believers who engage in profound reflection and, as a result, cultivate a life that bears enduring and meaningful fruit for the advancement of his kingdom.

December 30: Affirm my strength, resilience, and inner peace

On this thirtieth day of December, embrace the lessons of the past, the opportunities of the present, and the potential of the future. Today, choose to let go of what no longer serves you and welcome positive growth into your life. Be a beacon of light, radiating kindness, love, and joy with each breath. You are creating a life filled with purpose, gratitude, and meaningful connections. I am open to the abundance of the universe and trust in the journey that lies ahead. This day is a canvas, and you are the artist painting a masterpiece of positivity, compassion, and self-discovery.

December 31: Celebrate growth, love, and positivity

As you pen down the final entry for this year, reflect on the incredible journey of growth, love, and positivity that has unfolded across these pages for you. Each day that you read it nurtured your mind with uplifting thoughts, paving the way for a new chapter in the coming year.

This year, you witnessed personal growth that has shaped you into a stronger, more resilient individual. You have embraced the power of love, both for others and for yourself. You have fostered connections that have added richness to your life. Through the daily doses of positivity, cultivate a mindset that sees challenges as opportunities and setbacks as stepping stones toward greatness.

As the clock ticks down to the final moments of the year, choose to celebrate the victories, big and small, that have marked my journey. Acknowledge the lessons learned, the friendships forged, and the strength discovered within. Each positive affirmation read has been a brushstroke on the canvas of your life, creating a vibrant and uplifting masterpiece.

Let's raise a toast to the person we've become, the lessons we've embraced, and the positivity that has illuminated our path. May the new year ahead be a canvas awaiting our colorful stories, filled with joy, success, and new adventures. Here's to growth, love, and an abundance of positivity in the year to come. Happy New Year!

I want to take a moment to express my heartfelt gratitude to everyone who has purchased this book. My goal has always been to assist others on the journey we call life. I firmly believe that I was put on this earth to bring smiles to people's faces, and helping others has consistently been my passion.

I wear my heart on my sleeve, and it is this openness that fuels my daily motivation. I refuse to allow the challenges of this world to bring me down; instead, I am committed to uplifting those who follow my journey and everyone I encounter along the way. Every day, in my own unique manner, I strive to infuse a little more happiness into the world around me.

Thank you for being an integral part of my journey.

xo—YVETTE—xo

ABOUT THE AUTHOR

In the embrace of suburbia, by the ocean's edge, and amid the towering mountains, I relish the warmth of the sun on my face and the sensation of sand between my toes. Whether it's a cozy night by the fireplace or any other place, I discover inspiration and positivity. My heart belongs to a family I adore—four adult children and a loving family—with whom I cherish spending quality time.